FOOTSTEPS IN THE MUD

Dipo Toby Alakija

ISBN: 978 - 36348 - 9 - 5
978-978-36348-9-3

Printed in United States
Published by the publishing house of

CALVARY ROCK RESOURCES

19, Ajina Street, Ikenne Remo,
Ogun State,
Nigeria.

36, Thomson road
Gorton
Manchester
M18 7QQ
United Kingdom

270 Madison Avenue
Suite 1500, New York, NY 10016
United States

www.calvaryrock.org

INTRODUCTION OF "FOOTSTEPS IN THE MUD" BY THE PLAYWRIGHT, DIPO TOBY ALAKIJA

The episodes in this drama book are not mere fiction or literary works but series of stories that are based on various factual events. Although there are a few fictional materials which reflect in the dialogues, characterizations and ethnic backgrounds with the intention to make all the scenarios coherent and constructive but the entire works are the results of my research works into social vices, domestic and societal problems with numerous Nigerian cases that were studied. Some of these cases like a man who raised children and married two sisters of the same parents may prove difficult to believe but they are actually true.

The research works focus and trace the global problems from the development of the first group of people called Couple. Couple develops into another group called Family and then becomes chains of Families that turn into Community. The various groups of Communities constitute the entire society called State or Nation. All Nations on earth constitute the entire world.

The research works attempt to explain through dramatic forms various influences of individuals, families and society in the human lives, emphasizing on the importance of roles that are played especially by parents at home and teachers in schools. They are portrayed as role models that mold the entire society through young ones.

The episodes of the whole drama book may prove to be entertaining but the major aim is to educate, edify and inform everybody, especially adults and youths of the positive impact of their roles if they are well played and negative implications in the design of the future of the Family, Communities, Nations and the World at large if they are poorly played.

Through their attitudes and communications, youths and adults are reminded that they are either constructing a whole generation of God-fearing people or destroying the values that are required to make young ones responsible members of their respective families, communities and societies.

A lot have gone into the research works before the results are packaged in the form of this drama book. Hence, I wish to appeal to readers to study instead of just reading the book for fun and help me carry out my major aim by teaching others the lessons they would gain through each episode of the drama. I hope to share with adults, including parents, school teachers and Sunday school teachers, especially children and youth handlers a few things about our calls to duty and responsibilities in the epilogue of the story.

1

EPISODE ONE
GOING HAYWIRE
SCENE ONE

(Bosede goes to the tailoring shop with a nylon bag. Kola is in the shop, sowing some cloths.)

BOSEDE: Good afternoon, Mr. Tailor!

KOLA: *(stops working on his sewing machine.)* Aaba, Bosede! How many times must I tell you not to call me Mr. Tailor? My name is Kola.

BOSEDE: How can I call somebody of your age by name?

KOLA: See. As long as I'm not married, we are age mates.

BOSEDE: Really? *(She shakes her head with contempt and goes to sit close to his sewing machine.) Who said that to you? (She brings out the cloth from the bag.)*

KOLA: That is the truth.

BOSEDE: When people like you want to eat cow, they start calling it uncle.

KOLA: Whatever you mean by that?

BOSEDE: I have not come here for gist. I have come to sow these cloths. *(She shows him the parts of the cloths that need to be sewed.)* This place needs touching... and this...

KOLA: *(takes the cloth from her.)* You know I don't touch this kind of cloths. You're supposed to buy new ones.

BOSEDE: They are still new. I don't know how they got spoilt.

KOLA: Perhaps it's fake material you bought.

BOSEDE: It's not fake o!

KOLA: *(takes a bundle of cloths on a shelf.)* This is for you. I've been keeping it for you since the last time you came.

BOSEDE: *(looks surprised.)* You bought cloth for me? *(He nods, smiling at her.)* Why?

KOLA: Don't pretend as if you don't know why. I love you. That's why. All the while I've been telling you to be my girlfriend, you kept turning me down. Look, if you just say: "yes", I'll give you two thousand naira in my room right now.

BOSEDE: I'm not cheap girl!

KOLA: I know you are not. That's the reason I'm ready to spend so much just to win your heart.

BOSEDE: You know I want to go back to school.

KOLA: School? What do you want to do in school again? All other girls that graduated from secondary school with you are already married with children.*(He gestures at her.)* Here you are still thinking of going back to school.

2

BOSEDE: My parents want me to go to school, you know.

KOLA: You better leave your parents out of this and do what your mates are doing. *(He waves the bundle of cloth at her.)* **Are you taking this or not?** *(She slowly takes it.)*

BOSEDE: Thank you.

KOLA: What do you say about the two thousand naira in my room?

BOSEDE: You can go and bring it now.

KOLA: *(mimics her.)* "You can go and bring it now!" ... Just like that? What do you take me for? A fool who plants without thinking of how to harvest?

BOSEDE: What has planting got to do with the money?

KOLA: Don't tell me you don't understand me, bush girl.

BOSEDE: I don't understand.

KOLA: Let's go to my room. I'll explain what I mean to you.

BOSEDE: Kola, you want to play game...Eh?

KOLA: So you know it's a game after all. And you're pretending. *(He stands up.)*

BOSEDE: Well, I'm not a prostitute?

KOLA: Who says you are? After all, I've been telling you that you should be my girlfriend. Coming with me will only show you have accepted me as your boyfriend. *(He calls on his apprentice outside the shop.)* I'll be back soon. *(He looks at her as she stands up.)* Let's go, girlfriend. *(He and Bosede begin to walk down the street until they get to a house.)*

SCENE TWO
(Kola and Bosede lie on the bed, side by side in the room.)

KOLA: I don't know you know how to play this game. *(There is silence.)* And you do as if you're a village girl.

BOSEDE: Is that what I'm going to get for giving myself to you?

KOLA: *(tries to cuddle her but she takes off his hand.)* Oh, come ... Your know I love you.

BOSEDE: That's what you men used to say before you get what you want. When you get it, you begin to say all sorts of nonsense.

KOLA: You talk as if you've been dealing with a lot of men.

BOSEDE: *(looks at him sharply.)* Me? You don't really know me then. I only had one boyfriend when I was in school.

KOLA: One boyfriend is enough to make a man feel jealous!

BOSEDE: We are no longer together again. We parted our ways a long time ago.

KOLA: That's good. If you have to deal with me, I don't want any other man with you. If I see any man with you, I'll kill him with my hands. *(He shows her his fists. She laughs.)*

BOSEDE: Now that you're my boyfriend, where is the money you promise me? I have to go home now. My parent will be mad at me when I get home.

KOLA: Women! All they know is money. I'll give you while going.

(Mama Bosede and Baba Bosede are sitting beside each other outside the house. Baba Bosede reads the newspaper while Mama Bosede looks a little impatient.)

MAMA BOSEDE: Where in the world is this girl now? She's gone out since morning without looking back!

BABA BOSEDE: *(still looks at the newspaper.)* I thought she told you where she went.

MAMA BOSEDE: She said she wants to sow her cloths at the tailor's shop in Ajina street. That was hours ago.

BABA BOSEDE: Then why the hullabaloo?

MAMA BOSEDE: What do you mean by that?

BABA BOSEDE: It means you're barking like a dog.

MAMA BOSEDE: Don't you have anything good to say even for once?

BABA BOSEDE: *(looks briefly at her, adjusting his spectacles.)* You mean to say I never say anything good?

MAMA BOSEDE: Honestly, no! Since I married you for about twenty-five God-forsaking years ago, everything that always come out from your mouth is either destructive or abusive.

BABA BOSEDE: When do you ever do or say anything right since you were born? You're so foolish that you don't use your head before you talk. Imagine me reading and you barking beside me like a dog all because you have not seen your daughter.

MAMA BOSEDE: I suppose you didn't take the medication that is supposed to treat your mental illness.

BABA BOSEDE: It's your father that's mentally ill.

MAMA BOSEDE: You're from the linage of the lunatic. Everybody in the town knows that. *(With that, she stands up angrily and moves towards the front door of the house.)*

BABA BOSEDE: A lunatic slept with your mother before you were born, according to the history of your family.

MAMA BOSEDE: *(looks at him.)* God damn you and your linage!

BABA BOSEDE: Don't forget that your child had become part of the damned linage. *(Mama Bosede hurries inside.)*

SCENE FOUR

(Baba Bosede continues reading as Bosede walks to him.)

BOSEDE: *(half kneels down.)* Greeting to you, dad.

BABA BOSEDE: *(looks at her, removing his spectacles.)* Where are you coming from?

BOSEDE: I went to visit my friend.

BABA BOSEDE: When did you leave this house and why are you returning now?

4

BOSEDE: *(looks impatient.)* Oh, dad, you can't keep on treating my like child. I'm now grown up.

BABA BOSEDE: I see... You've grown up, eh? Because you've grown up, you feel you can do whatever you like? I know you'll follow your mother's footsteps. The business of prostitution that ruined her is what you want to start - right?

BOSEDE: Daddy, I'm not a prostitute! How can you say I'm a prostitute?

BABA BOSEDE: You're talking to me like that ?

BOSEDE: Why not? You call me and mummy prostitutes. *(He stands up, running after her with the determination to beat her. She begins to run round the place. Mama Bosede comes out when she hears noises. She pauses to look at them running after each other. Baba Bosede falls down. Mama Bosede begins to laugh at him.)*

MAMA BOSEDE: Look at him - elderly fool! Agba Iya! *(Baba Bosede goes to sit down, panting heavily.)* Look at you - good for nothing, shameless man!

BABA BOSEDE: Both of you are leaving my house today.

MAMA BOSEDE: Which house am I leaving? The one you built or the one we built together?

BABA BOSEDE: How much did you contribute to build it?

MAMA BOSEDE: No matter how small, we built the house together!

BABA BOSEDE: I know what to do to you. *(He looks at Bosede.)* As for you, go inside the house, pack your things and go back to where you're coming from. *(He shows her his five fingers.)* I give you five minutes to do that. After the minutes, anything can happen.

SCENE FIVE

(Uncle Wale comes out of the house with a walking stick.)

BIODUN: *(comes out also.)* Papa! Papa!

UNCLE WALE: *(looks at him.)* What is it?

BIODUN: You're going out without eating your food.

UNCLE WALE: Oh, I just want to stretch my legs. You know I've been sitting down since.

BIODUN: Why not eat now before you go out?

UNCLE WALE: If I eat now, I'll be too heavy to move.

BIODUN: So where are you going now?

UNCLE WALE: I just want to stroll down to my brother's house in the next street.

BIODUN: Please, don't take long. Unless you want your food to get cold.

UNCLE WALE: Keep it warm for me. I'll be back soon. *(He begins to walk down the street with the walking stick.)*

SCENE SIX

5

(Baba Bosede is still sitting down as Mama Bosede stands in front of him. They are screaming at each them.)

MAMA BOSEDE: You're a disgrace to the entire community! See, see... *(She waves at him.)* An educated person like you doesn't even know how to control himself yet he wants to rule his house! You expect everybody to respect you but you'll not respect yourself!

BABA BOSEDE: *(looks at her angrily.)* Look, woman, you're getting on my nerves! If you don't keep your dirty mouth shut, I'll strangle you to death with my bare hands!

MAMA BOSEDE: You can kill me if you can! All your mates are in high positions because they are responsible but, look at you, a retired civil servant that turns into bulldog that is biting everybody including his only child!

BABA BOSEDE: *(waves at Bosede angrily.)* You call that girl my child? Was it not in cause of sleeping around with different men that you came across her?

MAMA BOSEDE: Oh, oh! What is that? What are you trying to say? You mean she is bastard?

BABA BOSEDE: She is a bastard just as you are a bastard! You conceived her while you're prostituting!

MAMA BOSEDE: The so-called prostitution pays off then! If not for that, I'll probably not have a child at all because I'm married to the man who has no bullet in his chambers!

BABA BOSEDE: *(looks angrier.)* Today is the last day of your miserable life! *(He stands up suddenly and rushes inside the house and comes out with a cutlass a moment later. When Mama Bosede sees the cutlass, she takes to her heel. Just then Uncle Wale comes.)*

MAMA BOSEDE: *(goes to duck behind him.)* Help, Olori Ebi! Your brother wants to slaughter us!

UNCLE WALE: *(looks stunned for a while.)* Aaba! Baba Bosede! What is wrong with you? *(Baba Bosede stops chasing them when he sees him.)* Give me that cutlass this minute! *(He gives it to him.)* What is the meaning of this?

BABA BOSEDE: *(points at Mama Bosede.)* It is this woman! She's driving me crazy everyday. Ever since I married her, I have no peace of mind.

UNCLE WALE: It's okay. *(He waves to the chair.)* Let's sit down over there and talk about it. *(He looks at Bosede.)* You can get us more chairs. *(He goes to sit down on Baba Bosede's chair.)*

SCENE SEVEN

(Everybody except Bosede are sitting down There is silence between them.)

UNCLE WALE: ... So this is all what caused everybody to go haywire. *(He signs and shakes his head sympathetically before he looks at Baba Bosede.)* Why are you giving room for little things to effect your marriage,

Sunkanmi?

BABA BOSEDE: Calling me all sorts of names is not little thing to me, Egbon mi.

UNCLE WALE: You're thinking of what she said to you. What about the names you called her? You think calling a woman a prostitute and her daughter a bastard is something that will make her happy?

BABA BOSEDE: She said I'm from the linage of a lunatic.

UNCLE WALE: You feel using a cutlass to chase them around is the best way to prove her wrong? You can be the judge. She called you lunatic and you chase her with a cutlass.

BABA BOSEDE: *(looks away from him in a grudging manner.)* Egbon mi, you're taking side with her...

UNCLE WALE. *(looks at Bosede.)* You go inside. I'll talk to you later. *(Bosede goes inside the house. He stares at Baba Bosede.)* You're going to feel the length of my tongue if any of you say a word again. *(There is silence.)* What's wrong with you, Sunkanmi? When are you going to be matured? If you had your child early enough, you should be nursing your grand children, if nor great grand children by now. If you want people to respect you, you have to learn to respect others. No matter who they are. You just imagine how the whole thing begins. Bosede went out since morning, her mother expressed frustration in the way typical women always do. Instead of you to share or at least understand her frustration, you said she's barking like a dog. You don't realize the fact that for every action there is a reaction. Besides that, there is certain level of madness in everybody. When she reacted to what you said to her, things begin to fall apart and the center can no longer hold. *(He is silent for a while.)* Please, I beg you in the name of the Lord. Learn to be tolerant and patient with everybody, especially your household.

BABA BOSEDE: Okay. thank you, sir.

UNCLE WALE: You can go and talk to your daughter. Do the proper interrogation and give her proper discipline she needs before she can learn. I have to talk to your wife.

BABA BOSEDE: *(stands up.)* Okay, sir. *(He goes inside.)*

UNCLE WALE: I don't want to tongue-lash you in his presence so as not to give him more reason to persecute you. You've acted very foolishly by calling your husband names. Supposing other members of the family were around to witness you saying we're linage of lunatics, what do you expect them to say or think of you? Give you a pat and say, "good talk?" *(Mama Bose looks remorseful.)* The wise adage in the Bible says a wise woman build her house but a foolish woman pulls her own down with her own hands. You understand what that means, don't you? *(Mama Bosede nods and goes on her kneels.)*

MAMA BOSEDE: I'm so sorry, Olori Ebi.

UNCLE WALE: I'm not the one that needs your apology. It's your husband that needs it. I know your husband to be a very intolerant man. It's hereditary. He inherited that kind of attitude from our father. It would take the grace of God to deal with it . The problem here is not just his person but about you too. It would take a very patient woman to manage a man like your husband.*(He pauses.)* Do you want me to teach you how you can handle your husband?

MAMA BOSEDE: *(eagerly.)* Yes, Olori Ebi.

UNCLE WALE: Come closer and let me whisper it to you. *(She draws close and he begins to whispers something into her ears. She nods vigorously as he whispers to her.)*

SCENE EIGHT

(Baba Bosede sits on the chair outside, listening to the radio. Mama Bosede comes out with a plate of food and goes to set it in front of him. As she does that, she kneels down.)

BABA BOSEDE: What do you have here?

MAMA BOSEDE: *(opens the plate, smiling at him.)* It's your favourite, honey.

BABA BOSEDE: *(puts off the radio and looks at her.)* Whatever has happened to you these days is nothing less than a major miracle.

MAMA BOSEDE: *(laughs and goes to sit close to him.)* You can say that again. *(She touches his check.)* Feel young, honey!

BABA BOSEDE: I know when women treat their husbands like this, they actually need something from them. I also know it is usually something expensive but I have to remind you that I am a poor retired civil servant.

MAMA BOSEDE: *(laughs again.)* I actually need something from you.

BABA BOSEDE: I know it! I said it! *(She laughs loudly.)* You've been making me feel special for the past one month because you need something. Now tell me what I am going to pay for the VIP treatment. I hope I can afford it.

MAMA BOSEDE: I know you can afford it. I'm asking you to give nothing but the love you once had for me when we first got married.

BABA BOSEDE: *(looks surprised.)* What?

MAMA BOSEDE: Yes! I want you to love and marry me again.

BABA BOSEDE: Is that all?

MAMA BOSEDE: That's all.

BABA BOSEDE: If that's all, that's not really a request. It's something you really deserve. *(He begins to wash his hands.)* Let me finish eating my food. You will see that I'm still strong as I used to be.

MAMA BOSEDE: Are you sure? *(She laughs.)* You know I'll defeat you in the fight. I'm far younger than you...

BABA BOSEDE: You'll see. *(He begins to eat.)*

MAMA BOSEDE: *(stands up.)* Let me go and prepare for the fight.

BABA BOSEDE: Prepare for round one to five before a knock out.

8

MAMA BOSEDE: We shall see. *(She goes inside.)*

EPISODE TWO
LUST AFFAIRS
SCENE ONE

(Baba and Mama Bosede are outside the house, chatting.)

BABA BOSEDE: The party was the talk of the town. No one knew the man borrowed so much money for the party. When his creditors began to chase him around, he came to me in the office for help.

MAMA BOSEDE: Did you help him?

BABA BOSEDE: You expect me to help someone who created false image of himself with the money he borrowed?

MAMA BOSEDE: *(chuckles.)* I trust my husband! Some times he can seem so heartless but he's very principled.

BABA BOSEDE: *(looks jovial.)* Who are we talking about?

MAMA BOSEDE: *(laughs.)* You! You think I cannot say it to your face. You can be so mean at times, you know?

BABA BOSEDE: *(pretends to be amazed.)* What?!

MAMA BOSEDE: Let me prove my point. How did the man feel when he left your office that day? Did he feel better for coming to you for help?

BABA BOSEDE: *(bursts out laughing.)* You're a witch, you know! It was as if you were there. You should have seen his face that day! I thought he would jump through the window of the tenth floor and kill himself. *(Both of them laugh together. They are still laughing when Bosede who dressed provocatively comes out. Suddenly he stops laughing and looks at Mama Bosede, pointing at Bosede.)* See, see, this girl again. *(Mama Bosede looks at her.)* What do you find wrong in the dressing?

MAMA BOSEDE: Well... Em... I don't know.

BABA BOSEDE: My dear, you mean you don't find anything wrong in the way she dressed?

MAMA BOSEDE: Not really. You know the way youths of nowadays dress is different from the way we dress those days.

BABA BOSEDE: Let me tell you what is wrong in the dressing if you can't see it. Supposing a man under the influence of drugs or something get attracted to her, what do you think can happen?

MAMA BOSEDE: A mad man would always act as one, no matter how a lady dresses.

BABA BOSEDE: You don't seem to get the point. How do you expect her to attract a responsible man with this kind of cloths if at all she is looking for a husband? Come on, talk to me. The adage says if you attract a woman with

9

a good dance, when she sees a better dancer, she would leave you and go after him. If you attract a man by luring him with his kind of cloth, he would throw you away after sucking your juice.

MAMA BOSEDE: Bosede, go back and change into a better cloths.

BOSEDE: Oh, mum, dad, you're just being old fashioned.

MAMA BOSEDE: Better do what you're told. Your father doesn't like that kind of cloth. So go and change it now.

BOSEDE: I don't have another cloth to wear.

BABA BOSEDE: When you were buying cloths in the market, didn't you see a better one.

BOSEDE: Most of the cloths are like this.

BABA BOSEDE: You mean there are no descent cloths in the market again? Is that what you are saying? *(He shrugs.)* There is no problem. I've made up my mind that I will not let you get on nerves again. Also you cannot get between me and your mother again. I know even if we force you to go and change that cloth, deep inside you, you're ready to advertise your body to any man who is ready to bid for you. But you must get this straight: the day I hear that you are pregnant is the day you will be handed over to the man that impregnates you. I don't care the kind of person he is. If he's irresponsible or even an imbecile, I don't care. He's going to be your choice for marriage. We'll take nothing from him as dowry. If he doesn't come to take you, we'll take you to him. Whether you face there is your problem. *(He waves her to go.)* Get out of my sight! *(Bosede shrugs indifferently and leaves.)*

MAMA BOSEDE: Don't you think that's harsh?

BABA BOSEDE: Hash? I mean every word. If she gets pregnant, nobody can make me change the decision.

MAMA BOSEDE: What I mean is that you can't conclude that she's mixing with some guys.

BABA BOSEDE: Well, I stand to be corrected if I'm wrong but I have my reasons for jumping into that conclusion.

SCENE TWO

(Kola stands by the veranda of the house, leaning on the brace and looking left and right. He sees Bosede coming. He quickly goes to join her, trying to hold her hands.)

BOSEDE: *(snatches away her hands.)* Leave me alone. Some people may be watching.

KOLA: Let them watch for all I care.

BOSEDE: I care! Someone may see us and go to inform my parents that I was seen with a man.

KOLA: And so? Is your father going to marry you?

10

BOSEDE: You don't understand, Kola. You see, they are old fashioned folks. My father especially feels offended at my modern way of dressing. Take a look at me. Do I look bad?

KOLA: Of course, not. This is the way I want you to dress, you know. You don't dress like the old donkeys. *(He looks at her round.)* You look cute and sexy, baby. I am anxious to have you, you know.

BOSEDE: We have to protect ourselves this time.

KOLA: Oh, no. I don't like using rain coat.

BOSEDE: *(looks irritated.)* Then I'll go back home.

KOLA: Okay, okay, I'll put it on.

BOSEDE: Do you have some in your room?

KOLA: Well, I think I have… em... one ….

BOSEDE: Let's go and see. If there is none, you'll have to go and get some from the chemist shop.

KOLA: Okay. *(They enter the house.)*

SCENE THREE

(Uncle Wale and Biodun are outside the house, standing and talking together.)

UNCLE WALE: It's now two days since I strolled out to see my brother. So when your mother comes, tell her I've gone to see Baba Bosede.

BIODUN: What do want us to prepare for you?

UNCLE WALE: When I return, we'll decide that.

BIODUN: What if we have to buy it. You know it's getting too late to go to the market.

UNCLE WALE: You're just like your mother. Anyway, you can cook whatever food we have in the house. *(He begins to stroll towards the street.)*

SCENE FOUR

(Mama Bosede is picking some vegetables outside the house when Uncle Wale comes to join her. When she sees him, she quickly goes to welcome him.)

MAMA BOSEDE: *(kneels down.)* You're welcome, Olori Ebi.

UNCLE WALE: How are you, Mama Bosede?

MAMA BOSEDE: I'm fine, sir. Thank you. I'm afraid Baba Bosede is not around. He went out with a friend.

UNCLE WALE: I see.

MAMA BOSE: *(gestures him to her chair.)* Please, sit down. *(She goes inside to take another chair while Uncle Wale goes to sit. She later returns with another chair.)*

UNCLE WALE: It's now two days that I came to this area. So I decided to stroll down and see you.

MAMA BOSEDE: Thank you for coming, sir.

UNCLE WALE: So how is your husband doing now?

MAMA BOSEDE: He's doing very fine. Can I get you some water?

UNCLE WALE: Oh, no. Don't start treating me like a stranger.

MAMA BOSEDE: I really don't intend to. But how about getting you kola nuts

UNCLE WALE: No. don't border yourself about anything anytime I come here. If I need something, I'll say it. You know this is my house.

MAMA BOSEDE: That's true. That makes me feel better.

UNCLE WALE: Now tell me about the attitude of your husband recently.

MAMA BOSEDE: *(bows as she sits down, looking grateful.)* I really need to thank you again for the wonderful advice you gave me the other day. His attitude has changed a lot though we still have some minor misunderstanding. I have learnt how to resolve it. In a nutshell, I discover that if I want to get the best from my husband, I must give him the best of me. If I want to get the worst of him, I can do my worst. In fact, as at now, it's like we just got married. We both compete to please each other. Even when Bosede whom he suspected is going wayward tries to come in between us, we have a way of putting her inside.

UNCLE WALE: I'm glad to hear that both of you are now living in harmony. But the issue of Bosede going wayward borders me.

MAMA BOSEDE: I think the girl is doing fine. *(Just then Bosede comes home. She goes to greet them.)*

UNCLE WALE: Bosede, my daughter, how are you?

BOSEDE: I'm fine, sir. *(She half kneels down. She makes attempts to leave.)*

UNCLE WALE: *(beckons at her.)* Come here, young woman. *(She moves closer to him.)* What is this you are wearing?

BOSEDE: Oooh…. It's the latest design in town.

UNCLE WALE: *(nods thoughtfully.)* Hmm…. It's the latest design in town, huh? No wonder your father thinks you're growing wayward. *(He pauses and sighs.)* Bosede, I don't have you to blame. You can go inside. I'll talk to you later. *(Bosede goes inside. He looks at Mama Bosede who looks rather patient.)* You said the girl is doing fine.

MAMA BOSEDE: Yes, sir. I thought so.

UNCLE WALE: Back in those days, what do we call people that dress the way she did?

MAMA BOSEDE: Times have changed, Olori Ebi,

UNCLE WALE: Times have changed for better or for worse?

MAMA BOSEDE: I don't know what you mean, Olori Ebi. It depends on how you look at things

12

UNCLE WALE: Perhaps you don't understand what it means for your daughter to dress like this. She is telling a man outside there that she's available. How can a girl under your roof dress like that without you feeling something has gone wrong? Look, my wife, you don't need anyone to tell you that she is going out with a man. Even if she's not, she is about to. Dressing like that is intentionally meant to attract men to herself - the dressing implies that men are free to come and have a taste of her. You had two problems before now. You've solved one. The problem of your daughter going wayward is the second problem you have to look into otherwise you will regret not teaching her morals. You will see what I mean with time. The Yoruba adage says that if the words of elders do not come pass in the morning, it will surely come to fulfillment in the evening.

SCENE FIVE

(Few months later, Kola is in his shop, sowing some cloths. His apprentice, John is ironing some cloth on the table.)

KOLA: You better hurry up with what you're doing and go to where I send you.

JOHN: Yes, sir. *(After a while, Bosede comes into the shop.)* Welcome, aunty Bosede.

BOSEDE: How are you, John?

JOHN: I'm fine, thank you.

BOSEDE: *(goes to sit close to Kola who smiles at her.)* Hello.

KOLA: Hello, my love.

BOSEDE: I've come to see you.

KOLA: I know. *(He stands up.)* Let's go to my house.

BOSEDE: No, let's have the discussion here.

KOLA: *(frowns.)* You sound upset. I hope it's not so serious.

BOSEDE: It is very serious, depending on your reaction.

KOLA: John… *(He waves at him to go.)* You can go to where I send you. You'll iron the cloths later. *(John leaves the shop. Kola sits down again, looks suspiciously at her.)* Well, I'm all ears.

BOSDE: I've missed my period.

KOLA: *(looks jovial.)* Which period?

BOSEDE: This is not a joking matter ooo! I'm pregnant.

KOLA: *(shrugs.)* Good for you.

BOSEDE: Good for me? What do you mean by that?

KOLA: I wish you safe delivery.

BOSEDE: What are you trying to say?

KOLA: I should be asking you that question.

BOSEDE: You are going to be a father.

13

KOLA: *(pretends to be surprised.)* Me? Father?

BOSEDE: Are you saying you're not responsible?

KOLA: Even if I am, go and get rid of the pregnancy. I'm not ready to be a father. Look at me. Do I look like someone who is ready to be a father? *(He snorts.)* I'll never be a father now. I don't need to tell you that.

BOSEDE: Didn't you know this before you start riding on me like a horse? Besides I kept telling you we should use prevention but you told me you don't enjoy it when you use prevention.

KOLA: Look, baby, I'm not in the mood to hear that kind of stories. I paid for the service I enjoyed, didn't I?

BOSEDE: *(jumps on her feet.)* What! You mean to say you consider me a prostitute while you slept with me?

KOLA: I didn't say that. I expect you to prevent unwanted pregnancy out of the money I used to give you.

BOSEDE: Tell me if I didn't tell you to use prevention.

KOLA: There are other ways you could play safe.

BOSEDE: We are not getting anywhere with this argument. What are we going to do now?

KOLA: I told you to get rid of it.

BOSEDE: I have to go to the hospital at Sagamu before we can find a capable doctor to handle the abortion, I need close to twenty thousand naira to abort the pregnancy, going by what my friend told me.

KOLA: Where in the world do you expect me to get that crazy amount of money from? Even if you sell me, nobody would buy me at that price.

BOSEDE: You're joking, you know. If you have to sell every member of your family, including your parents, you will have to do that and get the money for me!

KOLA: Why don't you go and sell your own family and raise the money? You're the one who is pregnant, not me.

BOSEDE: You are telling me now that you don't have the money, right?

KOLA: That's right?

BOSEDE: *(stands up.)* That's okay. I have about one thousand naira which I can give to a native doctor to help me.

KOLA: If you value your life, don't go to any native or quack doctor for help.

BOSEDE: Did I say I'm going for abortion there? I'm going there to get the charm that will turn you into a mad person or a zombie who I can order around.

KOLA: *(jumps on his feet.)* What? You can't do that to me!

BOSEDE: Why not? If you are so useless to me, I'll me make you more useless to your family.

KOLA: If you turn me into a mad person, who will cater for you? *(He cuddles her to himself.)* Look, look, my dear, I love you, you know.

BOSEDE: *(pulls away from him.)* I'm giving you three options. You have to take one. You either get me the money by all means even if you have to break into a bank or you get ready to become a father and husband or you go mad.

KOLA: Obviously, the last option is not an option at all. So if I can't get you the money, I'll opt for the second option. In any case, none of them is good at all.

BOSEDE: You thought you're sleeping with a woman who has no womb, don't you? That's probably the reason you don't expect me to get pregnant at all.

KOLA: I'll think of what to do, I promise. *(She waves impatiently and walks out of the shop.)*

SCENE SIX

(Bosede is setting the table in the sitting room as Mama Bosede studies at her movement.)

MAMA BOSEDE: Bosede... *(She beckons at her.)* Come here. *(She goes to her.)* Sit down here…. *(She gestures her to sit beside her.)* I observe something recently.

BOSEDE: What is it, mum?

MAMA BOSEDE: It is not something someone can hide.

BOSEDE: What is it?

MAMA BOSEDE: You're pregnant, aren't you?

BOSEDE: *(frowns.)* Why did you say that, mum?

MAMA BOSEDE: Is it true or not?

BOSEDE: It's not true!

MAMA BOSEDE: You can say that to someone who does not know the symptoms of pregnancy. But not to me.

BOSEDE: That's not true!

MAMA BOSEDE: Listen to me, daughter. You better tell me who is responsible so that I can handle the situation before your father gets to know. *(There is brief silence before she raises her voice.)* Are you deaf? I say tell me who is responsible?

BOSEDE: *(looks away from her.)* It's Kola.

MAMA BOSEDE: Which Kola?

BOSEDE: The fashion designer at Ajina Street.

MAMA BOSEDE: *(looks as if she does not hear her well enough.)* The man that used to sow your cloths?

BOSEDE; Yes, mum.

MAMA BOSEDE: Aaaaah! *(She jumps on her feet and holds her head with both hands.)* I am finished! *(She points at her face.)* You're an imbecile! A moron! If at all you want to date someone, must it be a poor tailor who can hardly feed himself? You see the children of Awolowo, Osibamowo, Adelowo, Odumusi, Owolana, Osinbajo, Orepitan, Sofola, Adesina, Odubela, Ariyo and so many rich families like that in Ikenne. You didn't flirt around with anyone in those families. You went to sell yourself to a common tailor! Tailor! Aaah! You're truly a bastard! You will suffer until you die!

BOSEDE: I won't suffer! And don't ever call me a bastard!

MAMA BOSEDE: *(glares at her.)* If I call you a bastard, what are you going to do?

BOSEDE: Then I'll say daddy was right to say you're a prostitute when you're young like me. *(Mama Bosede becomes so furious that she begins to beat her. There is noise in the house before she manages to run out of the house. Mama Bosede runs after her.)*

SCENE SEVEN

(Uncle Wale sits outside, listening to the radio when Bosede runs to him. Mama Bosede runs after her. Bosede goes to stand behind Uncle Wale who looks puzzled, putting off the radio. Mama Bosede kneels before him.)

MAMA BOSEDE: *(gets up.)* Good afternoon, Olori Ebi.

UNCLE WALE: *(looks puzzled still.)* What is wrong? Why are you chasing your daughter down the street?

MAMA BOSEDE: She's pregnant!

UNCLE WALE: *(looks shocked.)* What? *(He looks behind him and gestures Bosede to stand in front of him.)* Is that true, Bosede?

BOSEDE: Yes, I'm pregnant. *(She points at her mother.)* She's not angry at me because I'm pregnant. She wants to kill me because the man that impregnated me is a tailor.

MAMA BOSED: She's a liar!

BOSEDE: You're the one lying!

UNCLE WALE: Would you stop that nonsense this minute - both of you? *(He looks at them.)* I'm disappointed in both of you. *(He looks at Bosede.)* You're in for a big trouble when your father gets to know this. You can go home. I'll see you and your father later in the day. *(Bosede goes away. He looks at Mama Bosede.)* You can have your seat. I have to talk to you first. *(Mama Bosede sits down on the chair beside him, looking impatient.)* Mama Bosede, do you want to hear the truth?

MAMA BOSEDE: I already know what you're going to say.

UNCLE WALE: Tell me what you think I'm going to say if you know.

MAMA BOSEDE: I know you're going to refer to what you say a few months ago about regretting it if I didn't teach Bosede morals.

UNCLE WALE: So you still remember. So what are you going to say about that?

16

MAMA BOSEDE: I did my best.

UNCLE WALE: No, you didn't do anything close to anything good, let alone best. Consider what she said about planning to kill her because she is impregnated by a poor man. What do you have to say to that? You can't tell me she is telling lies. *(She does not respond. She looks downward between her clasped hands.)* Whatever Bosede has become in life is largely your fault. As a good mother, you own your child the responsibility to teach her the right thing through what you say to her, your conduct and general attitude. It's not enough to say one thing and be doing another thing. If your words do not match your conduct, you'll be seen as a hypocrite.

MAMA BOSEDE: Olori Ebi, you talk as if I told her to go and flirt around with a man.

UNCLE WALE: Did you teach her morals?

MAMA BOSEDE: I tried my best. God knows that. I use to take her to the Church since she was a child.

UNCLE WALE: Taking your child to the Church is good but that is not enough. The proverb says charity begins at home. You did not teach your child morals at all. That is the truth!

MAMA BOSEDE: How else do I teach her? Once a sheep had given birth to the lamb, learning how to bleat is left for the lamb.

UNCLE WALE: A sheep is an animal, remember? You're not an animal. So don't compare yourself with one. You did not teach your daughter morals through your conduct, what you say and how you relate with your family. The other time the girl put on indecent cloths, you didn't tell her. Now she's pregnant just as your husband envisaged, you are chasing her around the street. What is your problem, Mama Bosede? I'm getting sick and tired of all these. I don't know how much more of this nonsense I can take but before I give up.

MAMA BOSEDE: *(goes on her kneels.)* I'm sorry, Olori Ebi. I'm really sorry.

UNCLE WALE: *(looks thoughtful.)* What do you want us to do about the problem on ground now?

MAMA BOSEDE: To me, there's no problem. Baba Bosede is the one to decide what happens. Already, he had said that once she gets pregnant, she is already married to the man that impregnates her. Since she has chosen to carry the baby of her tailor, let her be married to him.

UNCLE WALE: Just like that?

MAMA BOSEDE: What else? You'll see that's what will eventually happen unless you can influence her father to change his mind. If he changes his decision, I would consider it a major miracle. I don't expect any form of ceremony before she moves to his place since she's carrying his baby.

UNCLE WALE: (sighs.) Well, we'll discuss this with your husband later.

MAMA BOSEDE: *(stands up before she kneels in front of him again.)* Thank you, sir. *(She leaves.)*

EPISODE THREE
FORCEFUL UNION
SCENE ONE

(Kola and John are in the shop, sewing some cloths when Bosede hurriedly enters. The rest stop working and look at her, startled.)

BOSEDE: Kola, you're in a big trouble!

KOLA: *(looks impatiently at John.)* You can excuse us. *(He brings out some money from his pocket.)* You can go and buy me the item for the suit in the market. *(John takes the notes from him and leaves the shop almost immediately.)* Have your seat and let's talk about it. I know it has to do with the pregnancy.

BOSEDE: This is not a matter we discuss while sitting. You promised to give me the money to get rid of the pregnancy but you didn't give me.

KOLA: I tried to raise the money. I couldn't. I need time to get it. Some customers who promised to pay me for my service did not pay up. Please, I give me time.

BOSEDE: It's too late.

KOLA: *(frowns.)* What do you mean?

BOSEDE: My mother and uncle have discovered I'm pregnant. *(Kola looks perplexed, opening and covering his mouth with both palms.)* So the child has come to stay. I've told them you're responsible.

KOLA: I told you I'm not ready for marriage.

BOSEDE: You can tell my family that when they bring me here.

KOLA: Aah! I'm dead!

BOSEDE: You don't need to die now. Just accept me as your wife and you will live. If you don't, then you're a real dead man. I don't want to be a widow before I get married. *(She touches her stomach.)* Your child here forms the basis of our marriage. That's what I've come to tell you. *(She goes away. Kola puts his hands on his head in deep regrets.)*

KOLA: Oh my God! What's happening to me? What am I going to do now?

SCENE TWO

(Mama Bosede comes into the house and find Baba Bosede in the sitting room, eating.)

BABA BOSEDE: Where are you coming from?

MAMA BOSEDE: I'm from Olori Ebi. Where is Bosede?

BABA BOSEDE: Is she not in the house? I left the two of you at home when I went out, remember? *(Mama Bosede goes to sit down, looking angry.)* What is the matter? You look upset.

MAMA BOSEDE: It's Bosede!

BABA BOSEDE: What about her? *(There is silence.)* Don't treat your daughter as your rival in the house. Just tell me what the problem is. We'll find a way to solve it.

MAMA BOSEDE: The girl is pregnant.

BABA BOSEDE: Hmm hmm… I see.... *(He continues to eat.)*

MAMA BOSEDE: *(looks impatiently at him.)* You are not going to say anything about this?

BABA BOSEDE: There is no need to develop high blood pressure because of that. I was expecting it and I have told you what consequence or solution is going to be. As soon as she comes, just tell her to park her things and leave this house. She's already married. What God has put together, let no man or parents put asunder. The only thing that can make me go mad - mad enough to kill someone - is for the person to come and tell me I should keep her under my roof. As far as I'm concerned, my responsibility to the girl ceased from now on. So don't border calling anyone into this matter if you don't want me to kill someone.

SCENE THREE

(Uncle Wale is coming out of his house when Bosede meets him outside.)

UNCLE WALE: I am just going to see your parents.

BOSEDE: When you told me to go home, I couldn't go there.

UNCLE WALE: Why?

BOSEDE: I don't know how my father will react if he knows about it.

UNCLE WALE: If you know what you have done is right, why are you not at peace with your conscience? Hear what the proverb says: an offender runs when no one pursues him. Anyway, let's go. We'll talk on the way. *(They begin to walk down the street, talking.)* I have blamed your mother for happened.

BOSEDE: Really. *(He nods.)* How do you know she caused the problem?

UNCLE WALE: I'm not entirely blaming her. You have your own share of the blame.

BOSEDE: How, baba? I really don't see my fault. The things mum and dad used to say to each other make me feel doing the wrong thing is a normal way of life right from the time I was a child. When mum discovered that I am pregnant, she called me names for not flirting around with boys from rich families. If the man responsible for the pregnancy is from a well-to-do family, I wont be having this type of problem. After all, I'm their only child. Giving birth to a child only makes her only child to become two.

UNCLE WALE: Bosede, Bosede… Hmmm… Everyone that is born into this world would need to get reborn into the world of good words and conduct otherwise he or she would go through needless pains. Just because your parents do not teach you the right thing through their conduct or lifestyles does not mean you should be wayward. Before you appreciate the implication of what you have done, you will need to give birth to the child....

SCENE FOUR

(Baba Bosede is reading the newspaper in the sitting room while Mama Bosede sits down silently, still looking angry. Occasionally, she claps her hands and hisses.)

BABA BOSEDE: You can see that I'm reading.

MAMA BOSEDE: How do you concentrate when the house is on fire?

BABA BOSEDE: *(frowns.)* Fire? I don't see any fire. If you see it, call the fire fighter to put it off.

MAMA BOSEDE: That's the problem I used to have with you. Ever since you resolve to go into your shell, no one is able to get your concern and attention to anything.

BABA BOSEDE: I told you I don't want to have high blood pressure. I've got my own life to live. Please, live and let live. I want to live and die in peace, not in peices. *(There is a knock on the door.)*

BOSEDE: *(stands up at once and goes to open the door. Uncle Wale and Bosede stands by the doors.)* You're welcome, Olori Ebi. Please, come in, sir. *(Baba Bosede stands up when Uncle Wale comes in with Bosede who stays close to the door.)*

BABA BOSEDE: Welcome, Egbon mi.

UNCLE WALE: Thank you. *(He goes to sit down beside Baba Bosede who takes his seat when he settles down.)* How is everything?

BABA BOSEDE: Everything is fine except that Mama Bosede is making a mountain out of a molehill.

UNCLE WALE: What does that mean?

MAMA BOSEDE: I've told him what happened, Olori Ebi

UNCLE WALE: That would make my mission here less difficult. *(He looks at Baba Bosede.)* Well, what are you going to do about it now?

BABA BOSEDE: I was waiting for the cheap whore to come and park her things out of my house.

UNCLE WALE: I've been talking to her as we were coming. What she told me proves that she's not entirely to be blamed? The unhealthy relationship between you and your wife in the past contributed to her problem.

BABA BOSEDE: Egbon mi, you know you're the one I respect most in the family and I always obey whatever you tell me. If not for you, my wife would not be with me. Our marriage would have long become history. I really appreciate all you have done to influence me in a very positive way. But today, I am going to offend you. No matter what you say, that girl... *(He points at Bosede)* ... is not going to stay under my roof. If she has to stay with her parents as I expect you to say, let her stay with you. You are also her father. She'll be saved with you but if you force me to accept her, I swear, I'll kill her before nightfall.

MAMA BOSEDE: Aaaha!

21

UNCLE WALE: *(gestures her to keep quiet.)* That's okay. *(He looks at Baba Bosede.)* What if the man refuses to accept her?

BABA BOSEDE: You can have her as your daughter or she can go anywhere she likes. I'm sure you will take her. I can't have her under my roof anymore.

UNCLE WALE: If this girl was in my custody before now, you know she'll not be like this.

BABA BOSEDE: *(looks frustrated.)* Egbon mi, I don't want to say things I'll regret. Please, tell the girl to park her things and leave my house. Period.

UNCLE WALE: *(looks at Bosede.)* You have to do as your father says. You can go to your room and pack few things you need for now. You'll come for the rest later. You'll take me and your mother to the man that impregnated you. *(Bosede nervously goes into the room.)*

<hr>

SCENE FIVE

(Kola looks thoughtful as John who occasionally looks at him as he arranges some cloths on the table.)

JOHN: Master, what's the matter?

KOLA: *(looks impatient.)* Which matter?

JOHN: I…mean you looked worried.

KOLA: Shut up your mouth and face your work.

JOHN: I'm sorry, sir.

KOLA: *(sees Bosede who carries her bag, Uncle Wale and Mama Bosede coming to the shop.)* Tell those people I'm not around when they come here. *(He goes to hide under the table. Bosede leads the rest into the shop, drops her bag on the table and looks at John.)*

BOSEDE: Where's he?

JOHN: He's gone out.

BOSEDE: We've seen him while coming. I… *(Mama Bosede enters the shop with Uncle Wale. John greets each of them.)*

MAMA BOSEDE: Where's he now? *(She looks at John.)*

JOHN: *(points at the table with his hand, indicating that Kola is under it.)* He has gone out, ma. *(He continuously points at the table.)* He went to see one… *(Mama Bosede looks below the table and sees him. She begins to pull him out roughly. John immediately leaves the shop.)*

MAMA BOSEDE: Come out, you rogue! *(Kola comes out while Uncle Wale goes to sit down.)* What are you doing under the table?

KOLA: Em… nothing … I'm just… looking for some cloths.

UNCLE WALE: How are you, young man?

KOLA: I'm fine, sir.

MAMA BOSEDE: By the time we are through with you, you'll no longer feel fine!

UNCLE WALE: I'm sure you have elders in your family.

KOLA: Yes, sir.

UNCLE WALE: If you ask them how stressful it is to grow old, they'll tell you. I want to appeal to you. Please, don't give us any stress. Just answer all the questions we ask you before we tell you what we came for. *(He waves at Bosede.)* Do you know this young woman?

KOLA: Yes… sir. …

UNCLE WALE: Who is she?

KOLA: She's Bosede.

MAMA BOSEDE: We know she's Bosede, you moron!

UNCLE WALE: Hey! Mama Bosede, keep your mouth shut. *(He looks at Kola.)* Who is she to you?

KOLA: She's my ... *(He scratches the back of his head, looking sideways.)* She's... em... my customer.

MAMA BOSEDE: *(screams at him.)* God punish you and your family!

UNCLE WALE: *(looks at her sharply.)* Mama Bosede! I say keep quiet! What's wrong with you?

MAMA BOSEDE: *(half kneels down.)* I'm sorry, Olori Ebi. *(She points at Kola.)* He doesn't seem like a gentleman at all. If we handle him like a gentleman, he will not cooperate with us.

UNCLE WALE: Let me handle the matter my own way. If it doesn't work, we'll bring in the police as you suggested.

KOLA: *(looks agitated.)* Police? I'll tell you the truth… Em… Bosede is my girlfriend… em…

UNCLE WALE: That makes things easy. She's pregnant. Do you know that? *(Kola hesitates, scratching the back of his head again.)* Are you responsible for the pregnancy? *(Again there is silence.)*

MAMA BOSEDE: Are you deaf?

KOLA: I don't know, sir…

MAMA BOSEDE: What is it you don't know? You don't know you're deaf or what?

KOLA: I don't know if I'm responsible for the pregnancy.

MAMA BOSEDE: *(looks at Uncle Wale.)* Did you hear that? *(She looks at Kola.)* Thunder will strike you dead for saying that!

UNCLE WALE: Mama Bosede, I don't like the way you are behaving. I'll order you out of this place if you say a word again. *(He looks at Kola.)* Young man, do you always sleep with her? *(There is another silence.)* Talk to me, young man or I'll ask her mother to bounce at you like mad person. Do you sleep with her?

KOLA: Em…Yes, sir…

UNCLE WALE: How come you don't know she'll get pregnant? *(He stands up.)* You can see that she has parked her things. She's all yours now. You can come and pay her dowry and do other things as the normal customary marriage later.

KOLA: But I'm not ready for marriage. Sir!

UNCLE WALE: If a man is not ready for marriage, he doesn't let himself

23

loose like a street dog. You are now married - whether you like it or not.

KOLA: *(respectfully.)* Let her stay with her parents until I'm ready for marriage

UNCLE WALE: You are not in the position to dictate terms.

KOLA: I'm no dictating, sir. I'm only suggesting.

UNCLE WALE: Your suggestion is not relevant. We can't afford to have a pregnant lady under our roof.

KOLA: I need to get ready things before she can come and put up with me.

UNCLE WALE: Who is going to take care of her before then?

KOLA: I'll be bringing things...

MAMA BOSEDE: *(looks at Uncle Wale.)* Olori Ebi, my patience with this man is running thin! Let me speak the language he understands by dealing with him ruthlessly.

UNCLE WALE: *(looks at Kola.)* You really don't have any choice here. You have to take her under your roof and cater for her if you don't want us to get the impression that you plan to go about impregnating other girls.

KOLA: I …. I won't do that, sir. I promise.

MAMA BOSEDE: *(glares at Kola as she gestures at Uncle Wale.)* If not for our family head here, I'll make sure I finish you in this town! We came here to tell you're already married. Don't you dare look or even think of ways to dodge your responsibilities as a to-be father.

UNCLE WALE: Mama Bosede, let's go. *(He looks at Bosede.)* We'll see you later. *(He and Mama Bosede leave the shop. Bosede goes to sit down after they have gone.)*

KOLA: *(calls.)* John! *(John enters.)*

JOHN: Yes, sir!

KOLA: I'm now married by force.

JOHN: *(smiles at him and Bosede who looks indifferent, occasionally, hissing.)* Congratulation, master.

KOLA: God will punish you for saying that!

BOSEDE: You better leave him out of this, okay? If you have done what I told you, none of these would have happened in the first place. You keep telling me there's no money. *(She mimics him.)* No money! No money! No money! Now you must look for money to take care of me otherwise I'll make every minute of your life miserable.

KOLA: You don't mean you're going to give me problems, do you?

BOSEDE: If you give me reason to regret being forcefully married to you, I'll give you problem - a very big one that will send you to your early grave.

KOLA: Aaaah! *(He glances at John who is staring at the two of them.)* What are you staring at? *(He waves at her bag.)* Take her to my home. *(John quickly goes to take Bosede's luggage while she takes her handbag. They leave the shop.)*

SCENE SIX

(Baba Bosede is still reading the newspaper when Uncle Wale and Mama Bosede come into the compound. Mama Bosede opens the door and let Uncle Wale inside before she follows him.)

BABA BOSEDE: *(stands up.)* Egbon mi, you're welcome.

UNCLE WALE: *(goes to sit down.)* Thank you. *(Mama Bosede goes to sit down as well.)* The adage says that we should drive away the wolf that threatens the flock before we tend to the sheep. *(He signs.)* We have forcefully given your daughter to the man as you decided but there's a whole lot of danger in that.

BABA BOSEDE: Egbon mi, I don't see any danger in that. That's the life she has chosen. Besides that, she would still get married either now or later.

UNCLE WALE: I want you to think of it. A girl that is supposed to be in school is married off just like that.

BABA BOSEDE: Like I said, that is the life she has chosen. You can't hold me responsible for that. We tried our best.

UNCLE WALE: You didn't do anything! You are supposed to add value to her before she's given away like a cheap commodity. How do you expect her to survive in this highly competitive world without skills or further education? Even if she is not rated as someone in the class of destitute, she would be among the economically disadvantaged citizens of Nigerian. You are educated. I expect you know this.

BABA BOSE: I don't think that is necessarily so, Egbon mi. We are in a capitalist country. If she can work hard enough, she'll make money.

UNCLE WALE: How many hard working people do you know that is making money? An average Nigerian is hardworking. But the truth is: hard work is not enough. If Nigerians are empowered economically and with information, an average Nigerian would be comfortable if at all he is not rich.

BABA BOSEDE: I happen to belong to the school of thoughts who feel the problems of Nigeria are Nigerians. Take a look at what Bosede did. She wouldn't say she lacked anything.

UNCLE WALE: She lacks a lot of things that make her life like that.

BABA BOSEDE: I wonder what these things are.

UNCLE WALE: She lacks home training and family values which make her go wayward. She's not equipped with information about the real life. You and your wife are supposed to give her these things before she could understand the true meaning of life. As if that is not bad enough, you force her into the marriage which she is not prepared for. When she now gives birth to a child, she would teach the child what she understands about life. This is how social vices begin in the society

MAMA BOSEDE: *(kneels in front of Uncle Wale briefly before she sits again.)* Thank you, Olori Ebi. You're really a sage. May you live long and be our head. I can see my fault but it's too late to do anything about it.

UNCLE WALE: *(looks at Baba Bosede.)* Sunkanmi. Do you see your fault?

25

BABA BOSEDE: As you know, Egbon mi, nobody is perfect. We've lived in ignorance in the past. But I still don't see the justification in what the girl have done. Besides that, our faults don't put things right.

UNCLE WALE: Okay. *(He stands up to go.)* You have to get the girl some money she would need to start a business. I'll contribute my part.

BABA BOSEDE: Where do I get the money from, Egbon mi? You know I'm a retired officer who counts on his pension to survive.

UNCLE WALE: That's an order from me. If you have to sell part of your land, you would do that and get Bosede what she needs to start a business. At least, she is entitled to it as a member of the family. Besides, you were planning to give her tertiary education before all these happen. *(There is silence as Uncle Wale makes for the door.)*

MAMA BOSE: *(stands up with Baba Bosede who sees him off.)* Thank you so much, Olori Ebi. We are very grateful to you.

SCENE SEVEN

(John and Bosede walk down the street to Kola's house.)

JOHN: You have to be soft with my master. You know he doesn't like trouble.

BOSEDE: Who likes trouble, John? Tell me now. You think I like trouble, eh?

JOHN: Nobody likes troubles.

BOSEDE: I don't like trouble but I get into trouble. Look at me now. I'm leaving my parents at home - a place of comfort. I'm now going to put up with him. *(She shrugs.)* Well, I don't have to react now but I'm going to show him the beast inside me if I have a taste of suffering.

JOHN: I will advise you to be careful with him.

BOSEDE: If you want me to take to your advice, tell him to take care of me.

JOHN: I trust my master for that. He will do his best. *(They enter the house.)*

EPISODE FOUR
THE IMPOSSIBLE WIFE
SCENE ONE

(Bosede with a big tummy is taking her meal in the room while Kola puts on his shirts. After a while, he goes to sit beside her, looking at her.)

KOLA: Where's my food?

BOSEDE: There's no enough in house for the three of us as you can see.

KOLA: What do you mean three of us? There are only two of us here.

BOSEDE: *(points at her heavy abdomen.)* How about the one here?

KOLA: Even with that, the money I gave you yesterday is enough to feed all of us for at least three days in this house.

BOSEDE: *(looks at him with a frown.)* How much did you give me?

KOLA: I gave you one thousand and five hundred naira.

BOSEDE: *(waves at him with irritation.)* Look at you - just take a look at yourself. *(She mimics him.)* I gave you one thousand and five hundred naira.

KOLA: You mean to tell me the amount is small? That's a lot of money, going by the present economic state of the nation. With that kind of amount, I can feed for a whole week.

BOSEDE: Even the most wretched person in Nigeria would need much more than that to survive for a week.

KOLA: You're saying the money is finished, right?

BOSEDE: You're not deaf, are you? In fact you would need to give me another money before you go to the shop this morning.

KOLA: *(begins to laugh.)* You're joking, right? *(He laughs again.)* If that's a joke, it's a very good one. As you can see, I'm not in the mood for jokes. Just get me my food and let me eat before I go to the shop.

BOSEDE: *(hisses.)* Who is joking? *(She continues eating.)*

KOLA: You mean you're serious? *(She hisses again.)* I'm finished. Look here, woman, you can't spend money like that! I have not even finished the work of the money I gave to you.

BOSEDE: Who cares?

KOLA: *(lays his hands on his head.)* Yeeeh, I'm done for! This woman would reduce me to nobody!

BOSEDE: Hmm… Look at him talking as if he's somebody. There is nothing to reduce in you because you're nobody and nobody you would be remain for the rest of your miserable life. *(Kola silently puts on his shoes, getting ready to go.)* How about my afternoon food? *(He is silent as she goes to block his way out of the room.)* Are you deaf? I say where is the money for the afternoon?

27

KOLA: Bosede, you have not finished eating the morning food, you are asking the money for the afternoon food. Are you doing this to drive me crazy? You're a either wicked or foolish woman.

BOSEDE: You're calling me names? I know a lot of names I can call you. I have rich collection of them if you want me to dish them out to you.

KOLA: Please, let me go and do the work of the money you just squander. I may be able to bring home money if I get my balance.

BOSEDE: Better wash your tongue next time.

KOLA: Yes, ma'am. Can I go now?

BOSEDE: How soon will I get the money for the afternoon? You know that I cannot afford to stay hungry in my condition.

KOLA: That's the more reason you should judiciously spend any amount of money I give to you.

BOSEDE: If you don't want me to get angry at you, just don't refer to the money again.

KOLA: Okay. I'll send John to buy some food items in the market if I make enough money in the shop. If I can't, I'll send him to buy Iya Kofi fried rice for you.

BOSEDE: Oh, thank you. I prefer Iya kofi fried rice.

KOLA: Iya kofi rice is costly. We can't afford to be eating that everyday.

BOSEDE: You know my condition now, eh? Please, my husband, olowo ori mi, even though you never pay my dowry.

KOLA: I have to go now. *(He leaves the room as soon as she goes back to her meal.)*

SCENE TWO

(Mama Bosede comes out of the room while Baba Bosede reads the newspapers. He looks at her.)

BABA BOSEDE: I suppose you're going to the market.

MAMA BOSEDE: Yes. I'll check on Bosede and see how she's doing when coming back.

BABA BOSEDE: Okay. *(He continues reading.)* Make sure you are back on time to prepare my lunch.

MAMA BOSEDE: *(looks at him for a while.)* You don't seem to care about her or her condition.

BABA BOSEDE: *(without looking at her.)* As if I put her in the condition.

MAMA BOSEDE: She's our only child, remember?

BABA BOSEDE: You're telling me.

MAMA BOSEDE: You must understand that I am angry.

BABA BOSEDE: *(looks at her.)* Who are you angry at? Me or Bosede or her husband?

MAMA BOSEDE: Olori Ebi says we should not abandon the girl like that because she's not prepared for the condition she finds herself.

BABA BOSEDE: Listen, my dear. I've done all my brother wants me to do, which as you know is against my wish. Since the girl got herself impregnated by a man, let her face the consequences. My brother had forced me to cough out the money I cannot afford. I cannot do more than that. As you know, I'm trying to count my loss and recover from them. By telling me to do more, you are asking too much from me.

MAMA BOSEDE: I'm not asking you to do more. I'm only asking you to show more concern.

BABA BOSEDE: And what good do you expect from that? *(There is silence.)* Let me tell you what to expect. If you ask a frustrated man to show any concern in this circumstance, you are asking him to do his worst. I think my indifference is better than showing any concern if you ask me.

MAMA BOSEDE: *(sighs she goes to sit beside him, fondling his shoulder tenderly, as he leans backward.)* I'm sorry. I can't help thinking what Olori Ebi said. I think I have the lion share of the blame. I'm largely responsible for all the problems in my home. I realize it only when it's too late. I just need God to forgive me for frustrating my husband and for making our daughter irresponsible. *(She looks at him.)* I'm trying to make it up to you and Bosede though the foundation I laid for her is bad enough to affect many things about her life.

BABA BOSEDE: *(signs and part on her shoulder.)* We are both at fault but only you can make things up for her.

MAMA BOSEDE: *(sighs.)* I'll try my best but I'll need you to encourage me.

BABA BOSEDE: *(looks thoughtful for a while.)* I'll try to.

MAMA BOSEDE: *(stands up with smiles on her face. She kisses him on the cheek.)* Thank you. I'll go and prepare your favourite meal. *(She leaves the sitting room for the kitchen while he looks at her with little wonder.)*

SCENE THREE

(Bosede is on the bed, reading a book in the sitting room when John knocks at the door. He holds a bag.)

BOSEDE: Who is it?

JOHN: It's me, John.

BOSEDE: You can come in. *(John comes inside with the bag.)*

JOHN: Good afternoon, madam.

BOSEDE:. *(glares at him)* Why are you just coming?

JOHN: I have to go round the market to get the best price for each item, madam.

BOSEDE: *(frowns.)* Which items?

JOHN: Food items, of course. That's what my master told me to buy for you.

BOSEDE: You didn't buy me Iya kofi's rice?

JOHN: He didn't tell me to buy that, ma.

BOSEDE: *(looks angry.)* What?! Who did he expect to cook the food? Me? *(She points at her stomach.)* In this condition? Take the items back to him.

29

Tell him to give you the money to buy me Iya kofi's rice.

JOHN: *(looks reluctant.)* But madam you're not making things easy for my master.

BOSEDE: *(stands up to glaringly stare at him.)* And what is your problem about that?

JOHN: I feel you should take it softly with him.

BOSEDE: Shut up and do what you're told, you dummy. *(Just then Mama Bosede knocks at the door.)* **Come in!** *(Mama Bosede comes inside as she sits down. John greets her with a bow before he makes moves to go.)* Welcome, mum.

MAMA BOSEDE: Hello. Everybody... *(She looks at John.)* John... I believe that is your name.

JOHN: *(bows again.)* Yes, mama.

MAMA BOSEDE: I heard all both of you are saying. So you can put the items down and tell your master that she'll prepare the food. *(John obeys.)*

BOSEDE: Hmm, I won't cook any food! Gone are the days when you can order me around like little girl. You can't do that to me now - not here.

MAMA BOSEDE: *(looks at John.)* John, you can leave now. I'll talk to her. *(John bows again and leaves the room. She looks at Bosede and goes to sit beside her.)* We really have to talk, Bosede.

BOSEDE: I can't wait for the food to be ready. I'm starving.

MAMA BOSEDE: *(brings out some snacks out of the bag and gives her.)* You can take this before the food is ready.

BOSEDE: *(takes the snacks and begins to eat it.)* I still can't prepare the food. The bastard will have to come and prepare it by himself.

MAMA BOSEDE: We'll prepare it together when finished talking. *(Bosede continues to eat the snacks hungrily while her mother watches her, shaking her head pitifully.)*

BOSEDE: *(stops eating.)* Why are you looking at me like that?

MAMA BOSEDE: I'm just wondering how I can undo all the negative attitude you have developed through me and your father.

BOSEDE: What do mean?

MAMA BOSEDE: We'll talk when you finish eating. *(Bosede shrugs and continues eating the snacks.)*

BOSEDE: *(points at the table.)* Can you, please, get me the water behind that table? *(Mama Bosede stands up to get her the water.)*

SCENE FOUR

(Kola is sewing some cloths in the shop when John comes inside. He looks expectantly at him.)

JOHN: I've given her the items.

KOLA: She took the items from you?

JOHN: Yes sir. Her mother is there?

KOLA: *(frowns.)* What's the witch of a woman doing in my house again?

JOHN: I think she went to visit her.

KOLA: *(hisses.)* I'm sure she's there to teach her daughter how to make life terrible for me.

JOHN: I don't think so, sir. In fact if not for her, madam won't take the items from me. Madam told me to return it because she doesn't want to cook it. I was about coming with the food items when her mother came. She was the one that told me to put them down.

KOLA: *(looks thoughtfully.)* I see. If that be the case, I think the wind of change is about to blow. As the adage says: it's more difficult to tolerate impossible mother-in-law than a nagging wife. *(He starts singing as he continues sewing the cloths.)*

> **Oh my commanding wife**
> **She wants to destroy my life**
> **Oooooh aaaaah oooh aaah!**

(John begins to laugh. Kola glares at him.) What are you laughing at?

JOHN: *(stops laughing at once.)* I'm sorry, sir.

KOLA: Better be sorry for yourself. It'll soon be your turn to fell into the trap of a woman. I tell you. Once you are in, you can't get out of it unless you want to waste your life.

SCENE FIVE

(Bosede and Mama Bosede are together in the room.)

BOSEDE: *(snorts.)* Mum, you want to preach morals to me?

MAMA BOSEDE: It's not moral, Bosede. I'm telling you what can help you in your home. Very soon, you'll be raising children. The truth is: you're not prepared for marriage, let alone raising for children.

BOSEDE: You don't have to worry, mum. I am more than capable to handle my husband and children. I've learnt a lot from you. At least, I've seen the way you handled my dad. So I have what it takes to handle my husband.

MAMA BOSEDE: Listen to me, Bosede. The way I handled your father is not the right way.

BOSEDE: Whether it's right or not, at least it is effective. I'll use the method.

MAMA BOSEDE: There is far better way you can handle a man than that.

BOSEDE: Mum, I don't really need a lecture on how to handle my man. If I need one, I'll come to you.

MAMA BOSEDE: I can't let you to deal with your man the way I dealt with your father.

BOSEDE: Why not? If the method worked for you, it'll work for me for sure.

MAMA BOSEDE: *(looks impatient.)* It never worked! That is the point!

BOSEDE: *(looks indifferent.)* If you ask me, it worked. At least, he gave you your respect.

MAMA BOSEDE: *(looks puzzled.)* Do you mean to say the way we treat each other - the rains of obscenities, the open conflicts and the hullabaloo

31

are respects? What exactly is your own definition of respect?

BOSEDE: If you don't want me to call it respect, let me call it freedom then.

MAMA BOSEDE: That's not freedom. It's servitude. The consequence of All my wrong actions bring about his wrong reactions. You wouldn't be in this condition if I had played the roles of a mother well enough. Your father won't be so frustrated if I had played the role of a good wife. Things had been going wrong right from the onset. My failure as a mother is what is affecting you right now. We could not give you prosper home training because we lacked family values and ethics.

BOSEDE: Oh, mum, why are you telling me this now?

MAMA BOSEDE: I don't want you or your child to be faced with domestic problems. When a man is frustrated, he becomes violent even if he has a gentle personality.

BOSEDE: Mum, I really don't know what you want me to do now.

MAMA BOSEDE: I want you to have a good relationship with your husband. He seems like a good man. So you need to obey whatever he tells you.

BOSEDE: *(burst out laughing.)* Mum, I really can't believe you're saying all these. You want me to play the fool with a man? *(She laughs again.)* Why didn't you play the fool with dad at the early stage of your marriage with him? You're telling me to do what you cannot do. There is a word for things like that.

MAMA BOSEDE: What?

BOSEDE: You won't be offended if I say it? *(Mama Bosede shakes her head silently.)* People call it hypocrisy.

MAMA BOSEDE: *(signs and shakes her head slowly again.)* I have lost you a long time ago without knowing it. I can see that I'm no longer in the position to teach you the right thing. *(She shakes her head again before she looks at her.)* Let me ask you this: would you prefer the freedom to do whatever you like to the love of your husband?

BOSEDE: I prefer the freedom. I don't care if he loves me or not. If a man says he loves a woman, he's only looking for something. When he gets it... *(She points at her stomach.)* This is what the woman gets!

MAMA BOSEDE: You're wrong! That's the reason you're making the wrong choice. Even then, the so-called freedom has its own price tag. It can be so expensive that it can cost you your marriage with your husband and the peace in your home. He can go after another woman that promise him haven on her bosom.

BOSEDE: *(smiles.)* Mum, I may be your daughter but you don't have the faintest idea of who I am. If any woman messes around with him, someone would pay with his or her life.

SCENE SIX
(Uncle Wale sits outside his house as Baba Bosede goes to join him.)

BABA BOSEDE: *(bows how before him.)* Good afternoon, Egbon mi.

UNCLE WALE: Welcome, Sunkanmi. *(He looks towards the entrance to the house.)* Biodun! Bring a chair here.

BABA BOSEDE: I came here in the afternoon yesterday. I was told you were sleeping.

UNCLE WALE: Oh, yes. I was told. *(Biodun brings the chair, greeting Baba Bosede by kneeling down.)*

BABA BOSEDE: How are you, Biodun?

BIODUN: I'm fine, sir. Thanks you. *(She leaves after putting down the chair for him to sit. She goes inside again.)*

UNCLE WALE: How is Mama Bosede?

BABA BOSEDE: She's fine. She's the one that told me you want to see me.

UNCLE WALE: Oh, yes. I want to discuss with you the issue about Bosede.

BABA BOSEDE: *(sits down.)* I see. I hope you're not going to tell me to get her more money.

UNCLE WALE: *(chuckles.)* Oh no…. I just want us to discuss the type of business to set up for her.

BABA BOSEDE: Whether you decide is okay by me.

UNCLE WALE: That's another reason I call you. I expect you to show more interest in her. You always act as if I'm forcing you to do things.

BABA BOSEDE: Actually, you're the one making me do things for her. Left to me, she is on her own since the day she became pregnant.

UNCLE WALE: You know the adage that says that no matter how troublesome a child may be, you can't give him up to the tiger to devour. No matter what Bosede has done, she is still your daughter. You have to think of her future.

BABA BOSEDE: Okay, Egbon mi. *(There is silence.)* I suppose you have decided with her mother the kind of business she can do.

UNCLE WALE: We are thinking of getting her a shop where she can be selling different goods like canned food and things like that. We really need you to be part of the decision. So what do you say to that?

BABA BOSEDE: It's okay by me....

SCENE SEVEN

(Bosede is in the room, eating when Kola comes inside.)

KOLA: Hello, dear… *(She does not respond. He moves his shirt, leaving only singlet and pair of trousers.)* Where's my food?

BOSEDE: I cooked only my food.

KOLA: Why?

BOSEDE: It is because y has two horns and one long tail.

KOLA: You this woman, what exactly is your problem?

BOSEDE: I don't have any problem. It's you that has a problem - a very big one for that matter.

KOLA: Is there no more food in the house or what?

BOSEDE: I didn't buy and cook rice for the two of us.

KOLA: *(goes to sit down gently on the bed close to her.)* I don't know how long I can take this before… *(He shouts suddenly)*…. Go mad!

BOSEDE: *(looks at him indifferently.)* The state government has mad house at Abeokuta. Don't worry. I'll take you there if you run mad.

KOLA: *(holds his head with frustrations. Then he looks at her.)* Can you please tell me one thing - just one thing you want to achieve with this provocative attitude of yours? I've been in the shop working since morning. Whatever I make in the place, I bring it home. Now I can't even eat out of the food I bought with my own money!

BOSEDE: Blablabla…… story time. *(She hisses and continues to eat. There is silence for a while.)*

KOLA: Tell me, Bosede, what did I do wrong? Do I really deserve this treatment after all I'm doing to please you? Please, tell me.

BOSEDE: Okay, I'll tell you if you care to know. When I say I need something, you have to give it to me.

KOLA: What if I don't have it?

BOSEDE: You have to get it for me by all means.

KOLA: Even if I have to steal it?

BOSEDE: Yes! I don't care if you steal it.

KOLA: *(looks a little surprised.)* W-what? What if I get caught?

BOSEDE: That's your own problem.

KOLA: I can't believe this! What kind of wife are you?

BOSEDE: The wife that knows what she wants and knows how to get it from her husband by fire by force!

KOLA: Are you telling me now that before I can afford to keep you in this house as a wife, I must get you money by all means?

BOSEDE: That's the point.

KOLA: You may have to consider going back to your father's house.

BOSEDE: If you dare say a thing like that again or anything close to that, I'll see to it that you end up in a mad house. *(Kola stands slowly and goes to put his on shirt.)* Where are you going?

KOLA: Since I don't deserve the food in the house, I'll have to go out and look for something to eat before I'm starved to death. *(He leaves the room. Not long after that, Bosede begins to feel as if she is about to give birth to a child.)*

EPISODE FIVE
THE IRRESPONSIBLE HUSBAND
SCENE ONE

(Kola comes out of Iya Kofi's restaurant into the street, picking his teeth as he walks along. He meets Nuru driving a car on the way. He parks besides him.)

NURU: Kola, the tailor!

KOLA: Nurudeen, the mechanic. How are you?

NURU; I'm fine o...

KOLA: How is business?

NURU: Business is not too fine but we thank God.

KOLA: You have no reason to complain. All your customers are rich guys, going by the kinds of cars they ride.

NURU: Don't mind those rich guys o. They treat us like a road side mechanic. Instead of paying good money for the service we render, they would give us chicken change and tell us they'll give us bigger jobs.

KOLA: Still you get something big enough for your family.

NURU: Well, we thank God for that. How about you and your wife?

KOLA: So you know I've got a wife.

NURU: There's nothing hidden in this town, you know. We even heard that she would soon give birth. I hope you are getting ready for a big party.

KOLA: Big what?

NURU: Big party! I'll bring some guys to the naming ceremony. We'll drink beer that day until we get to the dead stage.

KOLA: You better save yourself that fantasy. Where do you expect me to get money to throw party around like that? You think we tailors make money like armed robbers the way you guys in the mechanic business do?

NURU: We'll give you a loan if you don't have money but don't tell us you'll not make a hell of noise out of the naming ceremony of your first child.

KOLA: You don't understand what I'm going through at home. If you do, you'll not tell me to waste the money which I don't have.

NURU: *(looks interested.)* What are going through, man?

KOLA: The woman I call my wife is determined to send me to my early grave.

NURU: Oh, boy, life is too good for any woman to shorten it for you.

KOLA: What am I supposed to do under this condition?

NURU: Prove it to her that you're the man of the house.

KOLA: How?

NURU: There are many ways to kill a chicken. I can teach you how to handle

35

the situation if you are willing to learn.

KOLA: I'm willing to learn o!

NURU: You deserve the best in life and you will get the best if you're willing to learn from guys like us. Anyway, where are going now?

KOLA: I'm going home but I don't feel like going now.

NURU: Why?

KOLA: I don't want to face that woman until night.

NURU: Then come inside the car and let's go to the beer parlour and enjoy yourself. *(Kola enters the car.)* I and the guys up there would teach you a few things.

KOLA: I don't have money to buy any beer.

NURU: Oh, don't worry about that. There are rich guys who will ensure that everybody drinks from the gay stage to the dead stage.

KOLA: What's gay and dead stage?

NURU: When we get there, you'll see. *(He drives the car out the place.)*

SCENE TWO

(Mama Bosede is in the house when Gbolahan knocks at the door.)

MAMA BOSEDE: Who is it?

GBOLAHAN: It's Gbolahan, ma. I'm one of uncle Kola's neighbours. *(Mama Bosede opens the door, talking with him by the entrance.)* Good afternoon, ma.

MAMA BOSEDE: Good afternoon. Can I help you?

GBOLAHAN: Aunty Bosede is in the hospital. She is about to give birth to a child.

MAMA BOSEDE: Aaah! Thank God! Is her husband with her?

GBOLAHAN: No, ma. We can't find him. That's the reason I have to come and inform you that she needs someone to be with her.

MAMA BOSEDE: What? You mean her husband is not in the shop.

GBOLAHAN: No, ma.

MAMA BOSEDE: Come inside and wait for me while I get needy to follow you there. *(Gbolahan enters the sitting room while she goes inside the bedroom.)*

SCENE THREE

(Kola is at the beer parlour with his friends. They all seem drunk as they chat.)

KOLA: I didn't know that this group of friends is as fantastic as this. *(He looks drunk as he sips more beer.)* If I had known, I would have been part of you since.

NURU: I told you about the group, didn't I?

KOLA: *(waves in a drunken stupor.)* Yeah, you told me.

KAYUS: *(looks at Nuru.)* Did you tell him about him about the Inner Caucus

36

Brotherhood?

NURU: Oh, no, I can't tell him that yet.

KOLA: Why not? I'm already part of you any time of any day.

NURU: How about your nagging woman?

KOLA: I now know how to handle her. I'll always prove it to her that a drunk is a punk! *(The rest roar with laughter.)* Before now if I sneeze like this... *(He sneezes.)* She would say: hey, pig, don't give me germs!

BELLO: She treats you like a leper?

KOLA: You get it, man. If I touch her and say, 'darling love me now', she would say, 'if you touch me, you will be sorry!'

KAYUS: She's your husband then.

KOLA: *(points at him.)* Man, you're damn right.

BELLO: How can you allow a woman to treat you like that?

NURU: I wonder o! If I am the one, I would turn her into punching bag. When I remove one or two of her teeth with one blow seven deaths punch, she would come back to her senses.

KOLA: I don't like to touch my wife like that.

NURU: That's the reason she's riding you like a horse like this... *(He demonstrates the way a horse is ridden.)* kutupa, kutupa, esin gongo! *(The rest laugh.)* You'll come and sleep in my house tonight and see the way I treat my wife. If my wife thinks she has mental problem, I'll prove it to her that I'm the father of all mad people in this town! *(The rest again laugh.)*

KOLA: Okay, I'll follow you home and learn how to handle my wife.

KAYUS: Good for you!

SCENE FOUR

(Sade sleeps on the couch in the sitting room as Nuru bangs at the door in the night, making her to jump up with a start.)

NURU: *(shouts from the outside.)* Open this goddamn door!

SADE: *(quickly goes to open the door and half kneels before him and Kola as they enter the house.)* You're welcome, sirs.

KOLA: *(looks a little sober, bows a little.)* Hello, madam.

NURU: Hey, Kola, why giving her the respect you cannot give to me?

KOLA: She seems like a nice and respectable lady to me.

NURU: So what?

KOLA: Respect is two way street. If she respects me, why shouldn't I respect her too?

NURU: *(looks at Sade.)* Where is my food, woman?

SADE: It's in the kitchen. It would have gone cold by now.

NURU: Why?

SADE: It's past mid night, sir. I prepared the food hours ago. I thought you'll come home earlier.

37

NURU: Are you questioning my movement or what?

SADE: You asked me why the food's gone cold and I'm trying to explain.

NURU: What did you cook?

SADE: It's rice and beans with fried plantain. That's what you told me to cook.

NURU: Well, I'm not bird or chicken to eat rice and beans. I want something solid like pounded yam.

SADE: *(looks a little worried.)* What?

NURU: You're not deaf, are you? I want solid pounded yam!

SADE: How do you expect me to pound yam in the middle of the night without waking the children and neighbours?

NURU: I told you never to argue with me again.

SADE: *(looks at Kola with appealing expressions.)* Uncle, can you, please, talk to your friend that it's not proper to... *(Nuru goes to slap her face. She screams sharply with pain.)*

KOLA: *(looks surprised.)* Nuru! Are you insane? *(Sade begins to sob.)*

NURU: I have told her times without number never to argue with me, let alone to report me to someone.

KOLA: Honestly, Nuru, I don't see anything wrong in what she has done or said. She's just trying to be rational here. Think of the sense behind what she said. There is no way she can pound yam at this hour without constituting nuisance to the entire neighbourhood.

NURU: I don't bloody care. I want pounded yam and I want it now!

KOLA: Be rational here, Nuru! As long as I'm here, you are going to be rational. You're going to eat the food she prepared.

NURU: *(looks thoughtful for a while.)* Because of you, we'll take the food like that. *(He looks at Sade who looks pitiable and a little frightened.)* I hope it's enough for the two of us. *(She nods with vigorously. He looks and smiles at Kola.)*

KOLA: Now you have to tell her you're sorry.

NURU: What?! Now it's you who is insane. The only thing I can do is to let her go and set the table. We'll eat the chicken food like that. *(He looks at her.)* Would you go and get us the nasty food you prepared? *(Sade goes into the kitchen.)* Don't forget to warm the shit before you bring here! *(As she leaves the sitting room, Nuru and Kola went to sit down together.)*

KOLA: I believe you have to tell her you're sorry.

NURU: You don't come here to teach me how to handle my wife. I brought you here to teach you how you should handle your wife.

KOLA: If I treat my wife like this, there will be war - I meal real war. She can even poison my food! I can never treat her like that come what may.

NURU: I can now see why she can order you around like a zombie. You're a fearful man. If you are a full member of our club, you'll have nothing to fear. Instead everybody around you will fear you.

KOLA: I'm not afraid of her. My conscience would be troubled if I treat her the way you treat your wife.

NURU: Then don't complain about her to anyone. Since you belong to the class of men that worship women, she has the right to ride you.

KOLA: Treating my wife with respect does not mean I worship her, you know. I can see that your wife is from a good home. If I'm married to a woman like that, we'll not be the same class. I'll be a good husband.

NURU: It's the way I handle her that makes her like that.

KOLA: I don't believe so. If it's my wife you treat like this, she'll go to a witch doctor and turn you into a crazy head.

NURU: Is that what she told you she'll do? *(Kola nods.)* How are you so sure she has not done that already?

KOLA: What do you mean?

NURU: If she has not done that to you, why treating her as if she is the boss in the house.

KOLA: I'm sure she didn't do that.

NURU: You believed her when she said she would turn you into a crazy man, don't you?

KOLA: Honestly, yes. That's the reason I often appeal to her not to do that by trying to treat her well.

NURU: Then I'm right to think you're afraid of her. The fear of what she'll do to you is the source of your problem. You know what, the Inner Caucus Brotherhood which the guys at the joint are trying to tell you about can give you so much confidence and boldness you would need before you can tackle her.

KOLA: *(looks interested.)* Really.

NURU: Yeah!

KOLA: Can they give me power to make money like you guys?

NURU: Oh, no but they'll give you powers to do other things and the connection with rich guys that will give you big contract. If you are a member, if at all you're not rich, you cannot be poor like an average Nigerian. The rule is that you must keep it a secret. You must not let anyone know what makes you influential and powerful.

KOLA: I see. No wonder you are hardly broke. The way you guys always spend money since I know you make me wonder how you get money.

NURU: It's not ritual money.

KOLA: I know. It's the connections that earn you money. If only I can get the connection through the group, most of my problem would disappear.

NURU: Yes, including the one posed by your wife

KOLA: Yes.

SCENE FIVE

(Mama Bosede carries the baby with her both hands, walking behind others as Gbolahan carries Bosede's bag. Bosede leads them into the

39

room.)

GBOLAHAN: I can't believe uncle Kola would not come and check you in the hospital.

MAMA BOSEDE: I don't know he's so mean like that.

GBOLAHAN: *(They enter the room.)* I don't know him with this attitude.

MAMA BOSEDE: Then something must be wrong with him.

GBOLAHAN: I believe so. I'll check him in the shop to find out.

BOSEDE: *(looks impatiently at him.)* I don't want you to see him for anything. He'll come to meet here. I'll trash out the nonsense by myself.

MAMA BOSEDE: I told you there is a better way to handle matters like this. You can't use hammer and chisel to handle a man.

BOSEDE: Mum, I honestly appreciate all you and daddy have done to bail me out of the financial problem in the hospital but I don't want you to tell me how to handle my husband.

GBOLAHAN: Madam, I suggest you take to the advice of mama.

BOSEDE: *(smiles at him ruefully.)* Thank you. I know how my mother would have handled the situation if she were in my position. I'm going to handle it exactly the same way and nobody - I repeat - nobody would teach me how to handle it.

GBOLAHAN: Aah… Please, madam, take it lightly o.

MAMA BOSEDE: *(looks at him.)* I'll talk to her. Can you do us one more favours, please?

GBOLAHAN: Yes, ma. Anything to be of help?

MAMA BOSEDE: You can help us look for Kola in the shop or anywhere you think he may be and tell him his wife had given birth to a baby boy.

BOSEDE: There's no need for that, mum!

MAMA BOSEDE: *(looks angrily at her.)* What's wrong with you? And what's wrong in doing what I just said? *(She looks at Gbolahan.)* You can help us look for him, please.

GBOLAHAN: All right, ma. *(He leaves the room.)*

MAMA BOSEDE: *(looks at Bosede as she goes to put the baby on the bed.)* I really have to talk to you this moment again.

BOSEDE: *(looks upset.)* We'll talk later. I'm too weak for anything now. I need rest.

MAMA BOSEDE: Okay. You can rest. I'll stay with you. When you wake up, we'll talk.

BOSEDE: Talk, talk, talk. I wonder what would come out of it. *(She goes to lie on the bed.)*

MAMA BOSEDE: *(begins to arrange the things in the room.)* I believe we'll get somewhere with the talk.

SCENE SIX
(Nuru talks with Kola in his shop while John presses some cloths.)

40

KOLA: I have never experienced the part of life you exposed me to yesterday.

NURU: You've not experienced anything yet. When you meet the brothers I've been telling you about, you'll understand why people like us can afford to do little work and get so much money.

KOLA: I'm really anxious to meet the brothers... *(Gbolahan comes into the shop.)* Gbolahan...

GBOLAHAN: Uncle Kola, we've been looking for you since yesterday afternoon.

KOLA: *(frowns.)* Why?

GBOLAHAN: Your wife delivered a baby boy.

NURU: *(looks excited.)* That's great news! *(He looks at Gbolahan.)* Young man, where are the mother and the child?

GBOLAHAN: They are at home.

NURU: *(frowns.)* She delivered the baby at home?

GBOLAHAN: They are discharged from this hospital this afternoon because there was no problem during the childbirth.

NURU: *(looks at Kola.)* Aren't you a lucky guy?

KOLA: *(looks a little indifferent, facing Gbolahan.)* I'll see them soon.

GBOLAHAN: Uncle Kola, don't do that. You have to follow me now. Your mother-in-law will be disappointed if you don't come on time.

KOLA: She's with her?

GBOLAHAN: What are you saying, Uncle Kola? If not for her running around to get all we need in the hospital and if not for your father-in-law who gave them money, how do you expect me to handle the situation in your absence?

KOLA: I'll come and meet them soon. Tell them I'm on my way.

GBOLAHAN: *(shrugs.)* Okay. *(He leaves the shop.)*

KOLA: *(looks at Nuru.)* I'm in hot soup.

NURU: What do you mean by that?

KOLA: Would you believe it if I say all I have with me right now is just fifty naira.

NURU: *(brings out some money from his pocket, counts it and hands it to him.)* That's five thousand naira. I expect that to take care of your immediate needs for now. I'll get you more later.

KOLA: *(looks surprised as he takes and he counts the money.)* This is a real surprise. I can't remember the last time I count so much money before.

NURU: That's no money. We call that chicken feeds. You'll get so much more by the time I introduce you to the brothers.

KOLA: I have to meet them.

NURU: Do you want me to follow you home?

KOLA: Oh, no, not yet. *(He shows him the money.)* With this money, I can handle the situation. I don't want you to witness the way my wife will treat me when she sees me.

NURU: You still haven't master how to handle her with all you have experienced so far.

KOLA: It'll take time before ....

NURU: *(interrupts him.)* ... before you take charge? You're not yet a man of the house but with time you'll know what to do.

KOLA: I'll try to do what you taught me. *(He stands up.)* I have to go now.

NURU: *(stands up too.)* I'll be going home too. We'll see later in the day at the joint. We have to begin to celebrate the birth of your son.

KOLA: Y-you know my condition.

NURU: Don't worry about the money. The guys will buy the drinks and pepper soup.

KOLA: *(They walk out of the shop together.)* I envy you, guys. *(As if it just occurs to him, he looks at John.)* If anybody asks of me, tell him or her I'm at home.

JOHN: Okay, sir.

SCENE SEVEN

(Bosede lies on the bed, looking up while Mama Bosede looks at her, still carrying the baby.)

MAMA BOSEDE: I thought you said you want to sleep.

BOSEDE: I cant, mum. I'm thinking of how to hit Kola where it hurts.

MAMA BOSEDE: You better don't think of doing anything stupid.

GBOLAHAN: *(knocks and comes inside.)* He's in the shop. I've delivered your message to him. He's on his way.

MAMA BOSEDE: Thank you very much, Gbolahan.

GBOLAHAN: You're welcome, ma. *(He leaves the room.)*

BOSEDE: When the lunatic comes here, I'll prove it to him that every normal person is insane.

MAMA BOSEDE: Don't call your husband names.

BOSEDE: Mum, did I tell you you piss me off with your moral lectures. Let me handle things my own way.

MAMA BOSEDE: You must understand that you make your husband whatever he is. So whatever decision you make, be ready to face the consequence.

BOSEDE: I'm ready to face it. *(There is silence before the door is knocked and opened. Kola enters the room. Bosede jumps up on her feet as soon as she sees him and goes to lock his shirt.)* You this animal, fungus face, lunatic, good for nothing, jinx! You left me through out the time I was in labour up to the time I gave birth to your own child! Goddamn your entire family, the lunatic linage of yours. (Mama Bosede holds her head, looking thoughtful as she recalls the time she also calls Baba Bosede names like that. Scene Seven breaks into flashbacks in scene three Episode One.)*

42

MAMA BOSEDE: ... I supposed you have stopped the medication that is supposed to treat your mental illness.

BABA BOSEDE: It's your father that has mental illness.

MAMA BOSEDE: You're from the linage of the lunatic. Everybody in the town knows that. *(With that, she stands up angrily and moves towards the door of the house.)*

BABA BOSEDE: A lunatic slept with your mother before you were born, according to the history of your family.

MAMA BOSEDE: *(looks at him.)* God damn you and your linage!

BABA BOSEDE: Don't forget that your child had become part of the damn linage....

(Scene Seven continues as Kola glares at her. He also recalls the time Nuru slaps Sade across the face as Scene Four Breaks into flashback.)

NURU: *(looks at Sade.)* Where is my food, woman?

SADE: It's in the kitchen. It would have gone cold by now.

NURU: Why?

SADE: It's past mid night, sir. I prepared the food hours ago. I thought you'll come home earlier.

NURU: Are you questioning my movement or what?

SADE: You asked me why the food's gone cold and I'm trying to explain.

NURU: What did you cook?

SADE: It's rice and beans with fried plantain. That's what you told me to cook.

NURU: Well, I'm not bird or chicken to eat rice and beans. I want something solid like pounded yam.

SADE: *(looks a little worried.)* What?

NURU: You're not deaf, are you? I want solid pounded yam!

SADE: How do you expect me to pound yam in the middle of the night without waking the children and neighbours?

NURU: I told you never to argue with me again.

SADE: *(looks at Kola with appealing expressions.)* Uncle, can you, please, talk to your friend that it's not proper to... *(Nuru goes to slap her face. She screams sharply with pain.)*

KOLA: *(looks surprised.)* Nuru! Are you insane? *(Sade begins to sob.)*

NURU: I have told her times without number never to argue with me, let alone to report me to someone....

(Scene Seven continues again. Kola removes her hand from his shirt, pushes her to the bed, showing her his fists as if he is ready to punch her.)

KOLA: If you come near me, I'll break all your bones! If you think that's a bluff, try me! *(Bosede gets up to face him but Mama Bosede steps between them.)*

43

MAMA BOSEDE: Kola! Kola! Has it gone to that level?

KOLA: Mummy, it's you I respect! If not for that, I would have beaten her senseless the moment she squeezed me with my shirt.

MAMA BOSEDE: You must not give the devil a chance!

KOLA: Please, leave the devil out of this.

MAMA BOSEDE: Why? Are you saying she has no right to be angry? You heard what she said, don't you?

KOLA: Yes, I heard all she said including calling me and family names. You heard her saying my family is of lunatic linage. I don't know of any man that can stand that insult unless he's truly a lunatic.

MAMA BOSEDE: *(in a soft voice.)* You've been away to God-knows-where through out the time she needed you most. She was in labour room for hours to deliver your baby. We look for you everywhere through out yesterday but we can't find you. If we had enough money to pay the bill, she is supposed to remain in the hospital. We have to run around to get everything she needed in the hospital which you're supposed to have bought before now. We did all that without you. Yet you think she doesn't have the right to be angry at you! You know this attitude does not prove that you're responsible. I'm not saying this because she's my daughter and I've been trying my best to teach her how to relate with you.

KOLA: *(bows briefly to her.)* I'm sorry, mummy. She's the one that pushed me to the wall. It was her nagging that pushed out of the house yesterday. I'm trying my best to please her but all I get is nagging, nagging all the time. I gave her some money to buy some food. After cooking the food yesterday, she did not give me out of it. So I went out to look for something to eat. The thought of coming back home to face her nagging was what kept me away from the house. She'll maltreats me and she'll not give me room to voice out my mind. She's doing everything to drive me crazy. I don't think I'll tolerate that for any reason - not any more.

MAMA BOSEDE: Things will change for good.

KOLA: I hope she changes because if she doesn't, she will begin to see the worst part of me.

BOSEDE: Things will not change if you don't care for me as I want.

MAMA BOSEDE: *(looks at her.)* You better shut up! *(She looks at him.)* I know you're doing your best. We all know the problem boils down on money. We're trying to open a shop for her where she'll be selling things. If you have more source of income, both of you will be comfortable.

KOLA: *(sighs.)* Okay, ma. Thank you. *(He brings out the money in his pocket.)* This is all I managed to get from a friend when Gbolahan told me she has given birth.

MAMA BOSEDE: *(smiles at him.)* You can have a look at your child. *(He returns the smiles as takes the baby from her.)* Let me have the money. We'll need to buy a few more things for the child and his mother. *(He hands the money to her with one hand, carrying the baby with the other hand.)* I know you're a good man.

44

KOLA: *(goes to sit beside Bosede who is still glaring at him.)* I'm sorry. *(He tries to reach for her but she pulls away.)*

BOSEDE: Leave me alone!

MAMA BOSEDE: You can continue to pet her while I go home now. I'll go to the market and get other items later.

KOLA: Thank you so much, Grandma.

MAMA BOSEDE: *(laughs.)* You're welcome. Take good care of her. I'll soon be back. *(She leaves the room while Kola tries to pet Bosede who still refuses to respond.)*

EPISODE SIX
THE BAD WOMAN BEHIND THE BAD HUSBAND
<u>SCENE ONE (A)</u>

(Sade is in the sitting room, helping the children with their homework when the door is knocked.)

SADE: Who is it?

BOSEDE: *(from outside.)* It's me, Iya Junior.

SADE: Please, come inside. *(Bosede enters the sitting room with Junior strapped on her back.)* Iya Junior, you're welcome.

BOSEDE: Thank you. *(The children go to greet her.)* How are you, children?

CHILDREN: *(at different times.)* Fine, ma. Thank you.

SADE: Now, children, you can go inside. As you can see, I have a visor. We'll continue the assignments later.

BOSEDE: There's no need for that. I'll soon be on my way. I only came to ask you if my husband was here.

SADE: I don't think he's in town.

BOSEDE: What makes you think so?

SADE: I heard him and my husband talking about going to Ilishan on a business trip three days ago.

BOSEDE: You mean your husband is not around too?

SADE: He's been away for two days now.

BOSEDE: *(frowns.)* And you don't have any reason to question or look for him?

SADE: Please, let's skip that part. *(She looks at the children who are still around.)* You can go to do your room. I have to talk to my friend.

BOSEDE: I really don't have much time to spend here.

SADE: I need to tell you a few things, please.

BOSEDE: *(shrugs and takes Junior who is few months old from her back. She goes to sit down.)* Okay. *(The children leave the sitting room.)*

SADE: *(goes to sit close to her.)* What I'm about to tell you can get me into serious trouble if you tell anyone. So I want you to first promise me you'll not tell anyone.

BOSEDE: *(hesitates.)* Why do you want do risk telling me in the first place?

SADE: It's going to help you in your family.

BOSEDE: I really don't see anything that can help me unless I help myself.

SADE: That's where you're missing the point. Don't try to play God in this matter. If you do, you're bound to fail.

BOSEDE: You heard what the Bible says that heaven helps those who help

46

themselves.

SADE: *(chuckles.)* Where do you find that in the Bible?

BOSEDE: If it's not in the Bible, it makes sense; considering the fact that God will not come down to help us.

SADE: You're right to think God will not come down to help us but he has people around us that can help. I see myself as one of those who can help you by telling the truth and facts about life.

BOSEDE: Okay, be my guiding angel then if God so desires.

SADE: First promise me you'll not tell anyone the secret about to reveal to you.

BOSEDE: I promise.

SADE: God is our witness because what I'm about to tell you would be said in good faith with the hope that it will help you. *(Bosede nods.)* Your husband used to tell my husband the way you always treat him. *(Bosede frowns.)* Yes. My husband used to teach your husband how to deal with you.

BOSEDE: *(looks thoughtful.)* I thought he's a nice man. He used to give my family lots of money.

SADE: *(smiles.)* He's not a nice man at all. In fact, if any good husband picks him as a friend, the good husband will turn into another thing in no time. But this talk is not about my husband. It's about you and your family.

BOSEDE: I noticed a lot of negative change in my husband ever since they became close friends.

SADE: Let me do the talking, please. *(She signs.)* If your husband develops the kind of attitude my husband's, you're in a very big trouble. Getting out of it would be near impossible. The question you're going to ask yourself is: "how did I get myself hooked up with a man like this?" *(She shrugs.)* Well, the man was my sister's husband when we were living in Ilishan.

BOSEDE: *(looks puzzled.)* Wait a minute. I don't understand. You mean your husband was your sister's husband? *(She nods.)* That's wickedness. How could you possibly snatched your sister's husband.

SADE: *(looks thoughtful.)* That's what people who don't really hear the whole story used to say. But the truth is: its' not entirely my fault. My sister has her own share of the blame.

BOSEDE: How can you possibly convince me?

SADE: I'll convince you by telling you the entire story. It will prove to you that there's always a woman backing a good or bad husband. The story will teach you how to handle your husband.

BOSEDE: *(nods vigorously with understanding.)* Okay, I'm all ears.

SADE: *(takes a deep breath as she begins the story with flashbacks coming in sequences.)* Before I got hooked up with Nuru, his marriage with my sister was somehow pleasant but she was not good at domestic work. So she brought me into the house. She told Nuru that she wanted me to live with them. At first he refused.

SCENE TWO
(Flashback)

(Nuru and Mary are sitting on a couch with Sade standing in front of them in a sitting room.)

MARY: I really need her in the house, darling,

NURU: Why? You want her take over your responsibility as the wife in the house or what?

MARY: Oh, no! I'm your one and only wife. But I need her here. She is very hard working. She can help us take care of the children and help me manage the restaurant business which we planned to have.

NURU: What would be your own duties?

MARY: I'll co-ordinate the works and also personally look after you. *(She playfully touches his check.)*

NURU: *(smiles and shrugs.)* Okay.

SCENE ONE B

SADE: Things went very well at the initial stage but my sister was so lazy that she left everything for me to do. She did nothing in the house and she did almost nothing to run the business of the restaurant where I have to work like a slave. I and Nuru complained to her but she would not listen to us. She wanted me to do the work alone or with Nuru and expected us to bring home money from the business. When business is dull, she would complain as if it was all my fault. The way she treated me in the house made Nuru to pay close attention to me and my needs. You know, one thing led to another before we became intimate. I sensed the danger in our coming together. So I decided to marry Dayo, a man that truly loved me. When he proposed to be my husband, my sister put her foot down and made sure I did not marry the man…

SCENE THREE
(Flashback)

(Mary and Sade are in the sitting room, arguing.)

MARY: I'll never allow you to marry that man, no matter what you do or say.

SADE: But why, Aunti mi? You know you're supposed to get me the best in life since you're the only family I have.

MARY: That's the very reason I cannot support your marriage with the man. You can never be happy with that kind of man.

SADE: *(looks confused.)* Why do you say so?

MARY: Can't you see him? He's as poor as Church rat.

SADE: I'll be happy with him. That's what that counts.

MARY: What do you know about love and happiness? Money matters in everything about life.

SADE: Including love?

MARY: Yes.

SADE: I don't think so.

MARY: I don't care what you think. You're not going to marry that man and that is final. *(She leaves the room.)*

SCENE ONE C

SADE: At first I thought she was really concerned about my welfare until I took another man to her.

SCENE FOUR
(Flashback)

(Mary sits opposite Sade and Dewale who are both sitting on the couch.)

MARY: Where do you work?

DEWALE: I work in a Micro Finance Bank in Lagos, ma.

MARY: If you marry her, you'll take her to Lagos?

DEWALE: Yes, ma.

MARY: *(looks at Sade.)* You want to go to Lagos with him.

SADE: *(nods with a smile.)* Yes.

BOSEDE: *(harshly.)* But you're not used to Lagos life and I don't want you to get involved with Lagosians.

SCENE ONE D

SADE: I didn't know immediately that my sister does not want me to leave her became I was very useful to her. While seeing the man off to the car park that day, he told me what he thought of my sister.

SCENE FIVE
(Flashback)

ADEWALE: I don't think your sister want you out of her sight. She wants to live your life for you.

SADE: Why do you say so?

ADEWALE: Do you note the way she reacted when I told her I'll take you to Lagos?

SADE: She's just being over protective.

DEWALE: Over protective sisters or mothers often times don't make marriages work.

SCENE ONE E

SADE: This is a fact. It soon dawned on me that my sister was actually thinking of herself alone. I became a very sad person. I cried almost every time. Strange enough, my sister was always so preoccupied in her interest that she didn't know or seemed to care about the pain she was causing me. Nuru noticed my mood one morning while I was serving the breakfast. My sister, of course, was still on the bed then.

49

SCENE SIX
(Flashback)

(Sade serves the table tearfully. Nuru sees her when he enters the sitting room. He goes to her. She tries to dry her tears.)

NURU: What's wrong, Sade?

SADE: *(forces a smile.)* Its' nothing, sir.

NURU: Then why are you crying if there's nothing.

SADE: I mean it's nothing to worry about, sir.

NURU: *(holds her two shoulders.)* Tell me what it is. I may not be in the position to help but you know I care. I can give you a good advice.

SADE: My sister keeps rejecting all the men I bring to her and I'm losing the opportunity to get a man that would marry me.

NURU: *(smiles.)* I see. You know you're a very lovely lady, hard working, well mannered, obedient and nice. I wish you're my wife because any man that marries you is lucky. Of course, every man wants to be lucky enough to have you...

SCENE ONE F

SADE: My head swells when he told me all those things. I became fonder of him when he told me how he appreciated me. Again, one thing led to another until I found myself on the bed with him.

BOSEDE: *(raises her eyebrows.)* You went to bed with him?

SADE: *(in a whisper voice.)* Yes. He took my virginity which I considered sacred to me. I had vowed that the man that took my virginity is the one I would marry. He was the first man to appreciate me and the only man in my life.

BOSEDE: You didn't remember he's your sister's husband, did you?

SADE: That's what frustration can do to a woman. I needed a man. I brought two different men but my sister kicked them out of my life.

BOSEDE: What you did to her does not justify what she did to you. You should have considered other options.

SADE: Like what?

BOSEDE: You could have run away from the house.

SADE: Again, that's near impossible. Nuru had really gone too far into my life when he took my virginity.

BOSEDE: And you decided to stay put in the house and give birth to the children of your sister's husband? That's madness.

SADE: Yes. A frustrated woman is a mad woman, you know. I'm not trying to justify my actions but I could have ended up in a psychiatric home.

BOSEDE: That's a better option if you ask me.

SADE: You may be right or wrong.

BOSEDE: What happened to your sister?

SADE: *(in a soft voice.)* She killed herself after she cursed the two of us that we'll never experience joy for the rest of our lives. *(Bosede looks so*

50

stunned that she could not say a word.) Since then, I've never experienced joy. When the talk about us was getting malicious in the town, we moved down here. Even then the curse is still in my family. It was in the cause of looking for solution to the problem that my husband came across the group that called themselves Inner Caucus Brothers or something. They pose as social clubs but the group is actually a secret cult.

BOSEDE: *(gawps at her in shock.)* I'm finished... Is my husband part of the group?

SADE: I don't think he's gone so deep enough to know that the group is a cult but he's part of them at the social level.

BOSEDE: B-but how do you know all these?

SADE: *(shrugs.)* I know so many things about my husband. I have a lot of his secrets which I can use against him but I dare not use it because I've been told in the group that I'll pay dearly for it if I do. If at all there's anything I have right now, it's my children and that of my sister.

BOSEDE: *(looks agitated.)* What?! You mean your sister had children for your husband? *(Sade nods sadly.)* How are you going to face it?

SADE: Face what?

BOSEDE: What are you going to do when your step children discovered in future that your sister was their mother?

SADE: We are trying our best to hide it. In fact I don't really know why I'm telling you all these secrets but, at least, you've given me your word that you'll keep it a secret.

BOSEDE: With the way the news must have spread around the town before you move down here and with your extended family's knowledge about it, how do you hope to keep it a secret? Let me tell you: they will discover the truth sooner or later.

SADE: *(shrugs.)* Even if they discover later in life, I would have tried my best to bring them up with the understanding that there are always two sides of a coin. I might have failed them one way or the other, at least, I try to make it up for them.

BOSEDE: Okay, okay. What do you think I should do about the case of my husband now?

SADE: You have to try to discourage his association with my husband and the group.

BOSEDE: I'm afraid that's almost two late now. My mother said something which I didn't believe until now. *(She looks a little thoughtfully.)* When I complained to my mother about his friends with the hope that she would persuade him to be more responsible to his family, she said I made my husband whatever he has become.

SADE: *(looks thoughtful.)* Hmm... Those are words of a wise mother. She is really right. I remember I complained bitterly when things were very hard for us. While looking for a way out of the problem, my husband got involved with the group. Your case is not is as bad as mine, you know. In your case, it's never too late or hard to get him. If you don't cut him off from my husband, you'll be the woman behind your bad husband.

BOSEDE: *(looks thoughtful for a long time before she stands up to lift Junior on her back.)* Thank you very much. You're truly a friend with you. *(Sade also stands up to see Bosede out of the house.)* I'll never forget this piece of advice.

EPISODE SEVEN
THE NAMES OF MY PARENTS
SCENE ONE

(Bosede helps Junior who is eight year old with his assignment in the sitting room.)

BOSEDE: ... Subtract means to remove. The question is: if you remove five from ten, how much would you get?

JUNIOR: Five

BOSEDE: Good. You can write five there. *(She points at the place in his book. Junior writes it. Just then Kola comes into sitting room, looking drunk. He staggers round.)*

KOLA: *(sings.)* Whiskey does it for me...
> What nobody can do
> Whiskey does it for me...

BOSEDE: *(looks at Kola briefly before looking at Junior who is smiling at him.)* Junior, you can go inside your room.

JUNIOR: Why, mummy?

BOSEDE: Would you keep quiet and do what I tell you? *(Junior goes towards the room and hides behind the door to listen to them.)* I've discovered that no matter how I try to clean the spot of a leopard, I can't succeed. I have tried everything I can to change you into a responsible husband and father but you keep proving it to me you're such a shameless man. Good for nothing and a jinx.

KOLA: *(in a drunken way.)* I expect you to call me more names. Let me call you your own names. Your names are lunatic, bastard, dunderhead head and the queen of imbeciles!

BOSEDE: *(looks angry and frustrated.)* Your family is cursed! I learnt that your grand father died of addiction to alcohol, your father died of the same thing and very soon, you'll end up like them. I don't have to wait for long before that happens. Now get this into your empty head! I'm going to do everything possible to stop you from transmitting the madness in your family to my child.

KOLA: It is your entire family that is insane, you know.

BOSEDE: My family? Every member of my family is responsible and you know that. If not for my parents who don't want me to move from one man to another, do you think I can stay put with someone like you - a mad man for that matter?

KOLA: *(still in drunken manner.)* Look at her feeling proud of her family who is a disgrace to the entire community!

BOSEDE: I'm not surprised at your attitude. I've always known that your

53

family is from a lunatic linage!

KOLA: Lunatic linage! I've told you I will kill you with my hands the day you say that to me again. *(He begins to move towards Bosede who quickly moves round the sitting room. She boos him.)*

BOSEDE: Shame on you! That drink will kill you one day. If it doesn't kill you, you will run into a truck, you will be crushed and you will die for good. That day we will have peace in the house!

KOLA: You're cursing me! I will kill you today. *(He runs again and falls down in a drunken stupor.)*

BOSEDE: *(jeers at him.)* Come and catch me if you can, useless man!

SCENE TWO

(Junior is in the classroom with other pupils as Miss Benson teaches them. Written on the board is the subject: Social Studies with Family as a topic.)

MISS BENSON: ...The nuclear family is made of what? Who can tell me? *(Some pupils raise up their hands.)* Yes. Moji tell us.

MOJI: *(stands up.)* It is made up of the father, mother and the children.

MISS BENSON: That's good. There was a time your parents were children like you. *(She points at Moji.)* They had names like you before they changed their names when they grew up. Now do you know the names of your parents?

MOJI: Yes, ma.

MISS BENSON: Okay, tell us.

MOJI: They are called Mr. and Mrs. Adeola.

MISS BENSON: I don't mean the family name. I mean their first names.

MOJI: I don't know that.

MISS BENSON: You can have your seat. *(She looks round at the rest as Moji sits down.)* I don't really expect everybody to know the first names of his or her parents. Is there anyone who can tell me the first names of his of her parents?

SEUN : *(rises up his hand.)* I can.

MISS BENSON: Tell me if you can.

SEUN: My mummy and my daddy call each other honey or darling.

MISS BESSON: *(smiles.)* That's not their real first names. These are pet names. You can have your seat. *(He sits down as she looks round.)* Who else would try? *(Junior raises up his hand.)* Yes, Junior, tells us the first names of your parents.

JUNIOR: I don't know if these are their first names but my parents used to call each other: Lunatic, Bastard...

MISS BENSON: What? Stop there! Where do you hear that?

JUNIOR: That's what they used to call each other every time they quarrel.

MISS BENSON: Oh, my God! Those are not their names. I don't want you to call anyone by that name again. Okay?

JUNIOR: *(looks confused.)* Why, aunty?

MISS BENSON: I would need to see you when we finish the class. I'll explain to you why. Do you understand?

JUNIOR: Yes, aunty.

MISS BENSON: You can sit down. *(Junior sits down.)* Who can tell me what extended family consists of? *(Again the some students raise up their hands.)*

SCENE THREE

(The Headmaster is in the office writing when Miss Benson knocks at the door.)

HEADMASTER: Yes, come inside. *(When Miss Benson enters the office with Junior, he looks up.)* Hello, Miss Benson.

MISS BENSON: Good afternoon, sir.

HEAD MASTER: *(waves at the seat in front of him.)* You can have your seat. *(She sits down silently while Junior remains standing.)* I suppose you're having problem with one of the kids, right?

MISS BENSON: The problem is not with him but with his parents.

HEADMASTER: *(leans background on the chair, looking at her and Junior.)* Well, tell me about it.

MISS BENSON: I asked the children to tell me the first names of their parents while teaching them about family. This boy, Junior started telling me all kinds of names his parents call each other. Names like lunatic, bastard... *(Headmaster frowns.)* Obviously, there is always rift between his parents.

HEADMASTER: *(signs and shrugs.)* Well, it looks to me as if you want to go into an issue that is none of our business.

MISS BENSON: I believe, sir, that it is part of our business as an individual and as a school to care for all children that are under our care. If we pretend as if it's not our business, the society would be affected.

HEADMASTER: You have that belief because you're a Christian. I appreciate you for that but you must understand that it is not a big issue to have conflicts in a family.

MISS BENSON: What makes it a big issue to me is that our moral lessons on family values in the School or Christian values at the School Bible Club Fellowship would be of no effect if we pretend as if the problem is not there. Besides that if parents sow negative seeds in the minds of their children, we are all going to reap the bad fruits as a nation in the nearest future because young ones, as you know, are the future of the nation. Whatever is sown into them now is what we are going to reap. Invariably, we are expected to mold our future through our children. *(She waves at Junior.)* From what this boy told me, there are always fights between his parents. What are they teaching him? To me, they are saying foul language and domestic violence is a normal way of life. When he's old, he can as well get involved in it.

HEADMASTER: What do you suggest we do now?

MISS BENSON: I'll like to see the boy's parents and explain the implications of exposing the child to such language and domestic violence.

HEADMASTER: I still maintain it that what is going on in his family is none of our business. Many people would not see things your way. Domestic violence is a common music we hear in so many homes every time. If you start going to many parents in their homes, they may think you're intruding into their affairs. They may not understand your good intention, going by what you went through before the PTA grant you permission to establish the Bible Club Fellowship. To teach parents of their responsibilities at homes is not part of our jobs, at least not in our job descriptions, even though I agree with you when you say we have the responsibility to design the future of the nation through young ones. You can do the little you can do through the School Bible Club without....

MISS BENSON: Oh, please, sir... *(There is silence.)* We only exaggerate the problem if we think the issue to too big for us to tackle. We can educate the PTA members of the need to put their children into considerations when engaging in foul language and domestic violence. You could use your influence among other educationists to campaign against this.

HEADMASTER: *(looks thoughtful for a while.)* Although I still feel some people are difficult to change, yet you are right. You make me see teaching as a noble profession through which we can mold the nation.

MISS BENSON: *(smiles.)* That's the point. We'll start the campaign against foul language and violence among parents right from the school.

HEADMASTER: I'll tell the PTA Chairman to give you time to talk to the parents during the next PTA meeting.

MISS BENSON: I'll be obliged to do that, sir. Meanwhile, I'll like to find time to see this boy's parents and let them know what happened in the school today. If I'm given the chance to tell them the implications of the frictions between them, I'll tell them. If they don't can hold my peace. I'll be glad if you can permit me to do that for mow, sir.

HEADMASTER: *(looks thoughtful for a while before he signs.)* It's okay but be careful how you go about it.

MISS BENSON: I will. *(She stands up, smiling at him.)* Thank you, sir.

HEADMASTER: *(smiles back at her.)* It's I need to thank for making me to see that we need to do more than giving them education. If we have a revolutionary teacher like you in every school in Nigeria, we won't have so much social vices that are attributed to broken homes in our society.

MISS BENSON: I'm flattered, sir. *(She smiles.)*

HEADMASTER: It is true. You can keep it up.

MISS BENSON: *(nods.)* I'll continue to the my best and leave the rest to God. *(She beckons on Junior to follow her as she stands up. They leave the office. The headmaster continues writing.)*

(Kola sleeps on the couch, snoring with a small bottle of dry gin by his side. Junior enters he room, looks at him and goes to take he bottle and examines it.)

JUNIOR: *(reads the label on the bottle.)* London dry gin. Oh... this is what the people drink in London... *(He opens the bottle.)* Let me drink part of it. *(He takes a gulp out of it and makes face.)* It's so bitter and burns in my mouth like fire. *(He looks at Kola who is still on the couch, sleeping and then glances at the bottle.)* It must be a sleeping medicine. That's the reason daddy sleeps like this all the time. I want to sleep like him. I'll take some more. *(He takes another gulp. He makes face again.)* Oowch! It burns inside my throat and stomach. *(He hears sound of someone coming.)* Mummy is back. If she catches me with it, I'll be in trouble. *(He quickly covers the bottle with the lid, put it back beside Kola and goes inside he room. Just then, Bosede comes inside the sitting room and sees Kola on the couch. She drops her handbag on the table, shakes head pitifully before she goes to tap him roughly at the back.)*

BOSEDE: Wake up, you this animal! *(Kola continues to snore. She pulls him angrily on the floor.)* Get out of here! Go and lie down in your family graveyard and die there! *(She taps him again.)* I say go and find somewhere else to die! *(He still does not move. She takes the bottle beside him, opens it and pours the content on his head. Kola wakes up with a start.)*

KOLA: *(in a drunken way.)* You this witch! You've come with your problem... Why do you pour water on my head now?

BOSEDE: See. See. Drunkard. You don't know the difference between water and swine urine. That's not water. It's the urine you've been drinking.

KOLA: *(looks a little sober.)* You pour swine urine on my head! *(He stands up clumsily.)* I'll kill you to day.

BOSEDE: *(moves away from him.)* Come and catch me if you can, foolish man! *(Kola hurries after her and falls down almost immediately. He stands up and falls again. Bosede moves toward the room.)* Come, come and catch me. *(He stands, moves and falls again until she leads him into the room. When he enters the room, she comes out and locks the door. She looks up.)* Oh, my God, when will this man change? He's growing worse everyday.

SCENE FIVE

(Bosede is picking some vegetables in the sitting room. She pauses for a while and frowns, looking at the time.)

BOSEDE: Where's this boy? *(She continues to pick the vegetables until there is a banging on the door of the room.)* Who wants to break the door there?

KOLA: *(roars from within the room.)* Would you come and open this goddamn door before I break it down?

BOSEDE: Break it down, you drunkard! *(She stands up to go and open the door.)*

KOLA: If I break it down, I'll break your head also! *(Bosede opens the door. He bursts out, looking angry.)* How dare you lock me up in the room!

BOSEDE: You were acting like an animal as you normally do when you're drunk.

KOLA: And so what? This is my house!

BOSEDE: Our house! We built it together, remember?

KOLA: How much do you contribute into the building?

BOSEDE: How much I contributed is not the issue here. The issue is we own the house together and you can't behave like animal here. I don't want Junior to witness the insanity in you. *(He begins to move away from her.)*

KOLA: Rubbish! *(He touches his shirt and looks at her.)* By the way how come whiskey smells all over my body?

BOSEDE: You're supposed to give me the answer to that. You must have bathed yourself with it. *(He goes to sit down silently looking thoughtful.)* Have you ever considered the implication of your attitude in this house?

KOLA: Look here, woman. Gone are the days when you were in charge of my life. I'm in charge of everything about my life now. I don't want you to ever question me about the way I behave.

BOSEDE: *(goes to sit down opposite him, looking at him.)* I have no faintest idea how I manage to live with a man like you for years without losing my mind.

KOLA: *(chuckles.)* You now regret having me as your husband?

BOSEDE: Regret is not the right thing to say. The right thing to say is how I manage to survive the agony you have caused me. I could have killed you or myself one day, you know.

KOLA: *(snorts at her.)* Why don't you kill yourself instead of me?

BOSEDE: I need to stay alive to look after my son. You're the one to die.

KOLA: *(hisses waves impatiently.)* I have no time for nonsense talk. Where is my food?

BOSEDE: Food is not ready as you can see.

KOLA: Now you see what I mean. You'll not give me food on time, you'll not give yourself to me so easily and I'll not get what I need without having to fight for it. Yet you expect me to change. *(He stands up and points at her.)* If there is any problem in my life and in this house, you're the cause.

BOSEDE: *(stands up to face him.)* You have the guts to point accusing fingers at me after all I've done to make our marriage work!

KOLA: What did you do!

BOSEDE: You're asking me? Let me refresh your memory. I gave you the money my parents gave me to set up a business. You said you needed it to execute a contract you got from the local government. When you returned the money, it was barely half of what I gave you. You said you're using it to build this house. When I started the business, I used all the gains to feed the family while you go about wasting money to get your self drunk! What else do you want me to do after all I did to change you? I know the real problem is the bunch of irresponsible friends you have.

KOLA: How dare you call my friends irresponsible! *(Just then Junior comes out of the room. They look at him.)*

BOSEDE: *(quickly goes to him.)* Junior. You're inside the room?

JUNIOR: *(in a drunken manner, he goes to sit down.)* I was sleeping like daddy when heard you.

BOSEDE: *(moves slowly closer to him.)* What's wrong with you?

JUNIOR: I want to be... like... daddy.

BOSEDE: *(looks at Kola briefly before she quickly goes to smell his mouth.)* Oh, my God! He's drunk! He smells of whiskey! Where did you get it from?

JUNIOR: It's something my daddy used to drink. I saw it there. *(He points at the spot.)*

BOSEDE: *(goes to lock Kola by the shirt.)* See what you have done to my son!

KOLA: *(looks upset.)* Why holding my shirt. Did I give it to him?

BOSEDE: *(unlocks him and goes to pull Junior with his hand.)* I'll nearly kill you today! Did I not teach you never to follow your father's footsteps?

KOLA: You better leave the boy alone if you don't want to cause more trouble.

BOSEDE: *(gives him a warning looks.)* You're the cause of all these. If you try to stop me from dealing with my child the way I want, this house would be too small for the two of us. *(She pulls Junior into the room while the boy cries for help.)*

KOLA: *(follows them into the room.)* You just said it now that I'm the cause. So leave the boy alone!

BOSEDE: You better stay out of this, useless man!

KOLA: *(pulls Junior away from her.)* If you don't leave him alone, I'll beat you until you're dead! *(They soon start struggling over the boy until Kola pushes her away.)*

SCENE SIX

(Junior is in the school with Lekan, standing and talking together.)

JUNIOR: Promise me you'll not tell anyone what I want to show you.

LEKAN: I'll not tell anybody, I promise.

JUNIOR: *(brings out a small bottle of whiskey and shows him.)* Here.

LEKAN: *(takes it from with.)* What's this?

JUNIOR: What's inside may be bitter and hot if you drink it but it will make you feel very good inside. *(Lekan looks reluctant.)* Come on, try it. *(Lekan opens it and tastes it. He spits it out quickly. Junior laughs.)*

LEKAN: Are we supposed to drink this?

59

JUNIOR: Yes! When you first take it, it feels hot and bitter but later you feel good and sleepy. *(Miss Benson comes from a corner and sees them. Lekan sees her. He quickly hides the bottle as she comes to join them. Both of them become silent.)*

MISS BENSON: What are boys up to? What are you hiding from me?

LEKAN: Nothing, ma.

MISS BENSON: You want me to use the cane before you tell me the truth? *(She stretches out her hand at him.)* Give it to me - whatever it is! *(Lekan reluctantly hands the bottle to her.)* And what is this? *(She opens and sniffs it.)*

JUNIOR: It's water.

MISS BENSON: It smells something else. *(She reads the label on the bottle.)* Water or whiskey? *(She looks at Lekan.)* Where did you get it?

LEKAN: Junior gave it me. He said it will make me feel good if I drink it.

MISS BENSON: *(frowns.)* Really? *(She looks at Junior.)* Where did you get it from?

JUNIOR: I took it from my daddy's room.

MISS BENSON: Do you normally drink it?

JUNIOR: *(quietly.)* Yes, ma.

MISS BENSON: How many times have you taken this?

JUNIOR: *(looks thoughtful.)* Four times. Ma.

MISS BENSON: *(shakes her head pitifully.)* Do you known what this can do to you?

JUNIOR: It makes me feel sleepy.

MISS BENSON: This thing can kill you.

JUNIOR: *(looks confused.)* But it didn't kill my daddy when he drinks it. It only makes him sleep all the time.

MISS BENSON: It kills slowly except you stop taking it. Every time it enters your stomach, it cooks everything inside you the way your mummy look meat. *(Junior and Lekan look surprised.)* If it continues to cook what it inside you like that, you will die soon enough. Do you want to die?

JUNIOR AND LEKAN: No, ma.

MISS BENSON: Then you must not touch it. Your parents are doing so many wrong things but I'll see and talk to them at home as soon as I can. As for the two of you, I want you to be members of Foundation Bible Club of the school. I'll teach you the way God wants us to live our lives. We'll read Bible and read stories from this book. *(She shows them the book.)*

JUNIOR: How can I get a copy, ma? I love stories.

MISS BENSON: You'll get one at the school bookshop. Before then, let us go to the Bible Club Fellowship. *(They walk together toward classroom.)*

EPISODE EIGHT
THE NEED FOR A CHANGE
SCENE ONE

(Miss Benson stands in front of the class, singing to the students. Junior and Lekan are among them, looking at her with rapt attention. She holds A-Z Foundation Bible Club Story Book in her hand. The song she is singing is written on the board. She points at each word with a small stick as the sings.)

MISS BENSON: *From day till night*
                                        I know God is by my side
                                        I know God will never leave me.

(She looks at the pulpits after she finishes singing.) The song is in his book. *(She shows them the book.)* Tell your parents at home that you need your own copy of Foundation Bible Club Story Book for the fellowship in the School. Okay?

PUPILS: Yes, Ma.

MISS BENSON: Now let's sing the song together. *(All the students including Junior and Lekan begin to sing the song. When they finish, she smiles at them.)* That's very good. Now clap for yourselves. *(They clap their hands.)* The title of the story we are going to study today is: Lola and the Bible. What is the title?

THE PUPILS: Lola and the Bible.

MISS BENSON; Good. Here goes the story. *(She looks at the book and starts reading.)* There was once a little girl in Nigeria called Lola. After she gave her life to Christ, her parents bought her a new children Bible. She never bordered to read it. She just put it on her reading table and read other books.

One day, she became so sick that she had to stay in the hospital for many days. The doctors and the nurses did all they could to make her well but the ailment became so serious that she thought she would soon die.

"Oh, Lord," she prayed, "please, don't let me die. I want to take care of my parents when I grow up."

Her friends from the school and the Church came to visit and pray with her.

One of them called Dotun read a passage in the Bible to her in Psalm 118:17. "I shall not die, but live and declare the works of the Lord."

"Did God say I will not die?" Lola asked quickly.

"Of course, yes," Dotun replied. "God will still use you to talk to others about Jesus. So you will not die."

61

"I was thinking I would soon die," Lola confessed.

"Oh, Lola, if you have been reading your Bible; you will easily know when the devil is talking to you."

"So if I don't die, I'll get well? " Lola asked.

"Of course, you're going to get well."

*Dotun said, "God has promised us many things in the Bible including good health." Guess what happened. Lola began to pray, using what she has read in the Bible to talk to God. She soon became well. From that day on, she always read the Bible. **(She looks round at the pupils.)** If you enjoy the story, let's give Jesus a locomotive clap offerings. **(She raises up her hands and put it down. As she does that, the students clap once. She does it again. They clap again. She does that continuously at intervals until the sound of the clapping begins to sound like a locomotive train that is about to take off up to the time the clapping sounds continuously.)** Now let us study the lessons in the story with the Bible. Who can tell me one of the lessons in the story? **(One of them raises up her hand.)** Tell us, Ayobami.*

AYOBAMI: The story teaches us to always read our Bibles.

MISS BENSON: That's correct! Let's give her a big round of applause. *(The pupils clap.)* Let us see passage that explains that in the Bible in book of Psalm, Chapter one hundred and nineteen Verse nine. Yomi, read the passage in your Bible.

YOMI: *(stands up to read the Bible.)* How can a young man make his way clean? It is by obeying your word.

MISS BENSON: Good! You can have your seat. *(Yomi sits down.)* The Bible says that all our wrong ways like disobedience to God and parents and other wrong things will be made right if we read the Bible. In that story, Lola did not know that it is wrong not to read the Bible. So when she fell sick, she thought she would die until her friends told her that if she had been reading the Bible, she would not think like that. Once again, let's give Ayobami another round of applause for giving us that beautiful point. *(Again the pupils clap their hands.)* Who else can tell us what he learns from the story? Junior, can you tell us?

JUNIOR: *(looks thoughtful for a while as he stands on his feet.)* I think it teaches us to have good friends.

MISS BENSON: That's another beautiful point. Let's give him too a big round of applause. *(The pupils clap their hands as he sits down.)* I am happy to hear that from you. There is another story in this book that also teaches that point. *(She waves the book to them.)* But the point I want you to get in this story which is not too different from what you said is that all children of God, including everybody here must always tell others what the Bible says. Let someone give Lekan his Bible. Lekan can read Psalm one hundred and nineteen verse thirteen. *(A pupil beside Lekan gives him the Bible and points the passage to him.)*

LEKAN: *(stands to read the Bible.)* With my mouth, I will say what God says.

MISS BENSON: Beautiful. That means we must always tell people about Jesus and what God says. Now, Lekan, can you tell us how we can know what God says?

LEKAN: Em... I don't know, ma. *(Many of the pupils immediately raise up their hands,)*

MISS BENSON: You know it, Lekan. We just studied it now.

LEKAN: *(looks thoughtful again. Then he looks excited.)* By reading the Bible.

MISS BENSON: *(looks excited.)* Excellent! Let's give him a very big round of applause. *(The pupils applaud him.)* You can have your seat. *(Lekan sits down.)* Who can tell me how Lola's friends knew that Lola had not been reading her Bible? *(Few pupils raise up their hands.)* I want a girl to answer the question. If a girl can't answer the question, it means the boys are the winners for today. Yes, Bimpe, tell us the answer.

BIMPE: Lola's friends knew she had not been reading her Bible because she thought she would die.

MISS BENSON: For saving the girls from being defeated today, let's give Bimpe a big round of applause. *(The pupils applaud Bimpe as she sits.)* If you don't read your Bible, you allow the devil to talk to you by thinking of many terrible things. The devil may tell you to go and steal but if you know the word of God, you will know who is talking. Lola thought of dying when the Bible says she will not die.

You all know what happened when Lola's friends taught her what the Bible says. She later believed she would not die and she became well. Let someone read the book of Psalm in the same chapter one hundred and nineteen verses eighteen.

SEGUN: *(stands from his seat to read.)* The passage says, "open my eyes to see wonderful things in your word."

MISS BENSON: Good! When you read the Bible, God will open your eyes to see wonderful promises God makes to all his children. If you believe the wonderful things in the Bible, they will all be yours. Lola believes she can be healed and she was healed...

SCENE TWO

(Lekan and Junior are walking together to their classroom, talking.)

LEKAN: Why is Miss Benson going home with you today?

JUNIOR: I don't know.

LEKAN: She may want to report you to your parents.

JUNIOR: She told me she has to talk to them for my own good.

LEKAN: That means she wants to report you.

JUNIOR: No. She just wants to tell them to lay good examples by doing the right thing.

LEKAN: That's good then.

JUNIOR: What do you think about what we learnt at the Bible Club today?

LEKAN: I love it. I didn't know the club is so good like that. And Miss Benson is so nice.

JUNIOR: Yes. She is very nice. I like her very much...

SCENE THREE

(The sitting room is empty when Miss Benson knocks at the door.)

BOSEDE: *(comes out of the kitchen to the sitting room.)* Who is it?

MISS BENSON: *(replies from outside.)* I'm Miss Benson, Junior's school teacher, ma! *(Bosede opens the door. Junior is stand with Miss Benson.)* Good Afternoon, ma.

BOSEDE: Good afternoon.

JUNIOR: *(prostrates to Bosede.)* Good afternoon, mum.

BOSEDE: *(frowns at Junior.)* Welcome... You don't use to greet me like that.

MISS BENSON: He just learnt that in the school today.

BOSEDE: That's good then. *(She waves them inside.)* Please, come inside. They enter the sitting room. *(She closes the door.)* Junior, you can go to your room and change from your school uniform.

JUNIOR: Okay, mum. *(He goes towards the room.)*

MISS BENSON: Junior.

JUNIOR: Yes ma.

MISS BENSON: Don't forget to pray for yourself and everybody before you do anything.

JUNIOR: Yes, ma. *(He goes inside.)*

BOSEDE: *(looks impressed.)* You seem to have specially influenced him.

MISS BENSON: Actually I was doing your job for you, ma.

BOSEDE: *(frowns.)* You can have your seat and explain what you mean. *(Miss Benson sits down silently and brings out her Bible.)* I hope you have not come here to preach to me.

MISS BENSON: I have come to tell you what can help you and your family. While doing that, I'll need to refer to the word of God. I hope you don't mind that, do you?

BOSEDE: *(in a polite manner.)* I really can't spare the time listen for now.

MISS BENSON: *(brings out a bottle of whiskey in her bag.)* But there's more than enough time to allow this in your home. *(She shows her the bottle.)*

BOSEDE: What's this?

MISS BENSON: It is something that has what it takes to ruin your family and that of other people in our school.

BOSEDE: *(sits down slowly and silently with puzzled expression.)* What does that mean?

MISS BENSON: We always have problems with so many parents who

64

would not listen to us when trying to point out the causes of the social vices in the society. When we suggest solutions, they will think we have come to make them religious people. That is why I was warned not to interfere with your family. But then, there is no way someone will not interfere, especially when the condition in your home is extending to other homes.

BOSEDE: I still don't get what is happening if you ask me.

MISS BENSON: *(shows her the bottle again.)* Does this belongs to your husband or not?

BOSEDE: *(looks confused.)* I don't know. If you tell me where you get it from, I'll be able to tell.

MISS BENSON: Junior brought it to school. He was trying persuade one of his friends to drink the content when I caught them. *(Bosede looks angry.)* You have no reason to be angry at the boy. He is only acting by what he sees around. What I need you to do now is to decide which of these you want Junior to pick as an influence in his life. *(She shows her the bottle of whiskey and the Bible.)* You don't need a prophet to tell you one of them would destroy his life while the other will construct it. You can decide which one you want us to talk about. In either case, I still have to preach to you. I either share the good news in the Bible with you or I share the bad news about your family with you.

BOSEDE: *(sighs.)* Tell me about the two, my sister.

MISS BENSON: That's a good idea. I'll start with the bad news about the condition of your family and the implications which you are yet to know.

BOSEDE: Before then, what can I get for you, ma?

MISS BENSON: This is more important to me than anything you want to offer. Can we skip that for now, please, ma?

BOSEDE: All right.

MISS BENSON: Thank you. *(She pauses.)* Let's have a word of prayer before we start. *(Both of them close their eyes and bow their heads as she prays.)*

SCENE FOUR

(Kola is sitting with Nuru in a compound, talking.)

NURU: The Brotherhood expects you to do certain things after making you financially comfortable. If you have done those things, you would be more financially buoyant by now.

KOLA: It doesn't look as if I got much from the Brotherhood.

NURU: You must not give anyone the impression that you're not grateful for all the members have done to connect you. We all know your condition before you join the group even if you have forgotten.

KOLA: I expected the Brotherhood to do more than to connect me with people that will give me contracts.

NURU: You should be grateful for what you have so far. At least you have your own house and enough money to be a man. If you have done all you need to do, your level would have changed by now.

KOLA: What are the things?

NURU: That's not for me to tell you.

KOLA: I hope the priest won't ask me to bring human beings or the blood of any member of my family.

NURU: *(laughs.)* Oh, no! That's far from the truth. By now, you are expected to know we are not into ritual killings of human beings.

KOLA: I know. Going by what is going on at the Brotherhood meeting I have attended so far, I have not experienced anything like that. *(He stands up.)* I need to go home and take my meal.

NURU: Hay, we can go to the eatery and take something together.

KOLA: Oh, no perhaps some other times.

NURU: *(also stands.)* Don't tell me your wife is still in charge.

KOLA: Far from it. When my son indicated it that he is following my footsteps, I feel should change a few things in my lifestyle.

NURU: You should be happy about that. Having a son that will emulate you is something you should be proud of.

KOLA: There is nothing to be proud of in some of the things I do. Do you want your son to take after you with all the atrocities you're involved in? If we have two of your type in this town, boy, there would be problems.

NURU: *(bursts into laugher.)* Am I so bad?

KOLA: *(walks towards the gate.)* Find that out from your wife. She knows you better than everyone!

SCENE FIVE

(Bosede and Miss Benson are talking in the sitting room with a bottle of soft drink in front of Miss Benson. She holds a Bible as she talks.)

MISS BENSON: Since the Bible instructs us in Proverbs Chapter 22 verse 6 that we should train up a child in the way he should go, God expects us to do our part which is to teach the children the right thing. When we do our part to teach children, God will do his part by ensuring that they do not depart from the right way. That is what that passage means. The problem we normally face in the school is that parents would not carry out their own responsibilities at home but they will expect God to carry out his own part. When God gives parents children, he doesn't give them armed robbers or cultists or prostitutes. They learn this in the world that is created for them. When they begin to give parents problems, they wonder what goes wrong, blaming God or the devil for the perverted lifestyles of their children. The truth is that: it's the parents that fail their children and God who gives them as blessing. When the children they are supposed to train with the word of God become menace, the nation and even the entire world begin to bear the consequences. They would cause problem and expect God to solve it. *(Kola opens the door and comes in. He pauses on the way when he sees them. Miss Benson stands up to greet him with smiles.)* Welcome sir.

KOLA: Hello... *(He looks at Bosede who is still smiling at him.)*

BOSEDE: Welcome, honey. *(Kola frowns. She looks at Miss Benson.)* This is my husband.

MISS BENSON: I guess as much.

BOSEDE: Can you join us in this discussion.

KOLA: I didn't come home for that. I'm hungry.

BOSEDE: The food is ready but you have to listen to what this sister is saying. She's Junior's teacher. Her name is Miss Benson.

KOLA: I see. You can't have hunger here... *(He points at his abdomen.)* And get sanity here... *(He points at his head.)* Nor expect this to work. *(He points at his ear.)*

BOSEDE: *(stands up to touch his cheek tenderly, smiling.)* She needs just few minutes of your time. This is important to me and Junior.

KOLA: *(shrugs.)* Okay. *(He goes to sit down. The two ladies also sit down.)*

MISS BENSON: Thank you, sir, for your attention. God bless you. *(She pauses briefly.)* Actually, I would have come here long before now to see both of you but I was much occupied. I have to find this time to come when I discovered that the longer I delay in coming, the more the problem in this family grows out of hand.

KOLA: What is the problem you noticed?

MISS BENSON: I asked the students in the class to tell me the names of their parents few weeks ago, Junior said your names are bastard, lunatic and things like that.

KOLA: *(half stands up.)* What? *(He looks at Bosede, sitting down again.)* That's your fault!

MISS BENSON: Sir, I've not come here to apportion blame to anyone but to suggest solution the problems in the family.

BOSEDE: I admit it's all my fault. I'm sorry. *(She looks at Miss Benson.)* You can tell him what also happened in the school.

MISS BENSON: *(takes the bottle of whiskey on the floor and shows it to Kola.)* Junior brought this to the school to share it among his friends.

KOLA: *(holds his head with surprise.)* Oh, my God...

MISS BENSON: Like I said I have not come to blame you but to advocate for a change. If Junior and other children are exposed to this kind of thing, how do you expect the society to look like? Please, tell me. *(There is silence.)* Social vices begin like this. So your life is not all about you alone. It is about your family, the nation and the entire world. If you don't have any other reason to change the negative attitude, you have your family, the nation and God who created you to think of. *(There is silence.)*

KOLA: *(signs.)* I'm sorry. *(He looks at Bosede and Miss Benson.)* I'll change.

MISS BENSON: *(smiles.)* Thank you. On behalf of your son who brought me here, your wife, the headmaster of the school who permitted me to come here and the entire society, I want to say thank you for that promise. It means a lot to every one of us. *(There is silence.)* Shall we have a word of prayer? *(They all bow down their heads in prayer. After the prayer, she stands up.)* I guess I have to go now. (Kola digs his hand in his pocket to bring out some money.)

KOLA: *(stretches the money to her.)* Please, take this for transportation.

MISS BENSON: Oh, no, Sir!

KOLA: I insist. Please, take it. You deserve much more if you understand what you have achieve here.

MISS BENSON: God does all good things. It's him who deserves all our appreciations. You can show it to him through positive attitude which you promise.

BOSEDE: *(looks at Kola who shrugs and pockets the money again.)* Junior is lucky to have a teacher like her. Don't you think?

KOLA: Yes, He's very lucky.

BOSEDE: *(looks at Miss Benson.)* Would you be our family friend?

MISS BENSON: Of course, yes! Why not? *(She begins to move out.)*

KOLA: *(looks at Bosede.)* You can see her off. I'll help myself with the food in the kitchen.

BOSEDE: Okay, dear. *(She and Miss Benson leave the house.)*

SCENE SIX.

(Bosede and Miss Benson walks down the street, talking on the way.)

BOSEDE: You have a way of touching the hearts of people.

MISS BENSON: I wish I understand what you mean, ma.

BOSEDE: I've never seen my husband filled with regrets since I knew him.

MISS BENSON: Only God can touch the hearts of people. Before coming to see you, I prayed to God to touch your hearts.

BOSEDE: God did answer your prayers. *(She looks at her briefly.)* You said you run a Bible Club in your school.

MISS BENSON: Yes, ma. It's called Foundation Bible Club.

BOSEDE: How do you run it? Do you compel students to be part of it?

MISS BENSON: Oh, no. We make it a voluntary program. The school always recommends it to parents as a way of boosting the moral values of young ones. You know, we have tried everything we can to equip the children spiritually and emotionally but we've failed to make the young ones godly people. The only thing that cannot fail is the word of God.

BOSEDE: You're right. Do you run the Club as a Church in the school?

MISS BENSON: *(laughs.)* Of course not! We meet once in a week to study from the book I told you about. There are stories, Bible lessons, songs, poems and class activities in the book. We always encourage parents to find time to have fellowship with us. You'll understand why you need to encourage it.

BOSEDE: I think it would be a good idea if I witness what you do there. I have a friend who has a very troubled family. Her children don't come to your school but I'll bring her with me when coming for a visit in your school. That may encourage her to bring her children to the school.

MISS BENSON: I'll love that very much.

BOSEDE: If she likes the way you teach the children the word of God, I'm sure she'll be encouraged. What time and day of the week do you normally meet?

MISS BENSON: We usually have it on Fridays at noon.

BOSEDE: *(looks thoughtful.)* We'll find time to come then.

SCENE SEVEN

(Miss Benson, Bosede and Sade sit in front of the class, looking at the children, singing and reciting the poem.)

JUNIOR: *(stands in front of the class to lead the students.)* Let us pray. *(They all closed their eyes.)* Father, we thank you for this day. As we are about to start today's Bible Club Fellowship be with us in Jesus' name.

THE REST: Amen!

JUNIOR: Let us recite the poem about heaven, which we studied last week.

THE REST:　　*H for heaven*
　　　　　　　The beautiful haven
　　　　　　　The home of people
　　　　　　　That follow the Bible.

JUNIOR: Let us sing the song about heaven

THE REST:　　*I belong to my Lord*
　　　　　　　He will take me to heaven
　　　　　　　He has built me a mansion
　　　　　　　He will not let me down!

JUNIOR: Before we ask our mummy in the Lord to tell us the story titled Heaven is A Beautiful Place, I want to read to you the book of Revelation Chapter Twenty-One Verse Four. *(He opens the Bible he is holding and begins to read it.)* And God shall wipe away all tears from their eyes; there shall be no more death, or sorrow, or crying. There shall be no more pains for the former will pass away. *(He looks at the students.)* That place is talking about heaven. The beautiful heaven where there is no pain or sorrow. Let us sing the song about heaven once again before our mummy come to teach us about heaven with the story from our book. *(The students sing while the ladies except Miss Benson look a little excited.)*

THE REST: *I belong to my Lord...*

SCENE EIGHT

(The headmaster is reading through some files when the door is knocked and Miss Benson leads Bosede and Sade into the office.)

HEADMASTER: *(stands up when he sees them.)* You're both welcome, ma.

69

BOSEDE AND SADE: Thank you, sir.

HEADMASTER: *(looks at Miss Benson.)* You're through with your Bible Fellowship.

MISS BENSON: Yes, Sir. *(She gestures at Bosede and Sade.)* As I told you, sir, they were with us through out.

HEADMASTER: I see. *(He gestures them to sit in front of him. They sit down when they all sit down, he settles down again.)* How do you find the Fellowship, ma?

BOSEDE: It's wonderful!

SADE: If someone told me the boy that leads the Fellowship at the beginning is my friend's son, I won't believe it.

HEADMASTER: *(smiles.)* I'm glad to hear that.

BOSEDE: Miss Benson had turn my son into a Pastor. My husband won't believe this.

SADE: All the children look so responsible and godly.

HEADMASTER: *(looks at Miss Benson who smiles with modesty.)* I think Miss Benson deserves the credit. She insisted that we have the Bible Club Fellowship in the school despite oppositions among some members of the PTA.

BOSEDE: You mean there were oppositions to a thing like that?

HEADMASTER: Of course, there was. The only argument against the idea was that: not all the children are from Christian background. That is the reason we always get the consents of the parents before we make them members of the Bible Club Fellowship.

SADE: Well, I'm bringing two of my children to this school because I want them to be part of the Bible Club Fellowship.

HEADMASTER: We'll be glad if you do that but we don't always recommend that.

SADE: Why?

HEAD TEACHER: Each school has its own strength. While some schools are very sound academically, some are sound in the moral aspect. There are some that combine the two but lack discipline. What we always advise parents is to make up for the weakness of their children's schools rather than to withdraw them and take them to another place. If you feel Bible Club Fellowship will help your children in the school, you can approach the school and ask for it. *(He stretches out his hands at Miss Benson.)* Can I have the Foundation Bible Club Story Book? *(Miss Benson gives it to him.)* You can recommend that this book can be used in the School Fellowship or to instruct young minds on moral issues. You can even use it even at home. Before you know it, the Bible Fellowship will turn into a Bible Club. I know of ten-year-old twin sisters that did something like that. They attended a big and old school that was established by a man who did not believe in God before he died. Many people who passed through the school died as atheists. It was difficult to share the gospel or anything that has to do with religion. So it was difficult for the twin sisters to tell everybody about Jesus in the school. They have been told in the Church that it is important to share the word of God with everybody. According to their testimonies, they prayed to God to give them the wisdom to share the word of God with their friends in the school without breaking the school regulations. They came across the book. They were so inspired by the book that they decided to be telling their friends the stories inside during the recess. They were able to attract all their friends with the stories. It soon became the habit of many of the pupils to gather in one place to hear stories from the book. Before the teacher got to know what was happening, the twin sisters have formed a small Bible Club where they could sing songs in the book, hear stories and even worship God in the school that was established by an atheist! If ten-year old children can be inspired by God to use a book to established a Bible Club in a school like that, I can't see reason an adult cannot.

SADE: *(signs and nods.)* I like your candid and unbiased advice but I still want my children under the influence of Miss Benson.

HEAD TEACHER: If that's your decision, it's okay.

EPISODE NINE
THE SPIRIT OF PAYBACK
SCENE ONE

(Kola drives to the front of the house with Bosede sitting beside him in the car. Mama sits at the back. Junior comes out of the house to welcome them.)

JUNIOR: *(waits beside the car for Kola and Bosede to come out.)* Welcome, mummy, daddy!

KOLA: *(opens the car door and goes to pat him.)* How are you, son?

JUNIOR: I'm fine. *(He goes to greet Bosede who hugs him.)* Welcome, mummy. Why do you take so long?

BOSEDE: Daddy's hometown is quit long, you know. How are you doing anyway?

JUNIOR: I'm fine. I just miss you.

BOSEDE: We've been away only a few hours, Junior.

JUNIOR: That's long enough, mum. *(He looks inside the car.)* Who's inside the car?

BOSEDE: It's Grandma.

JUNIOR: Grand ma! *(He opens the door and tries to pull her.)*

KOLA: Hay, be gentle with her. She's not feeling so fine.

JUNIOR: Oh, Grandma. What's wrong with you?

BOSEDE: She's not feeling very fine. We brought her here so that we can take care of her. You can get her things in the boot while we help her inside. *(She and Kola go to take Mama out of the car while Junior goes to take at her bags in the car boot.)*

SCENE TWO

(Mama eats with her hand shaking. The food falls on the table. As she attempts clean it, her hand pushes the plate on the table and breaks it. Kola rushes out of the room and goes to her.)

KOLA: *(stops to look at Mama, looking angry.)* How come you break the plate?

MAMA: I ... I didn't do it intentionally.

KOLA: Why are you doing things like a baby, Mama? Are you a baby?

BOESEDE: *(comes out. Mama silently rests her head on her left hand.)* What's wrong?

KOLA: Mama just broke the plate that cost me a lot of money to buy.

BOSEDE: It's okay. Everybody makes mistakes.

KOLA: You don't call that a mistake. The plate was on the table. I don't know

72

how she threw it on the floor.

BOSEDE: *(looks upset and pulls him aside.)* I really don't like you talking to your mother like that. *(She moves closer to Mama while Kola goes back inside the room.)* I hope you are not hurt, Mama.

MAMA: *(silently.)* No, my daughter.

BOSEDE: I'll get Junior to clear this place. *(She goes inside.)*

SCENE THREE

(Mama is the kitchen, using a stick to walk; looking for a cup. There is a plate on the fridge. She tries to remove them but it falls down from her hand and breaks. Bosede rushes inside. She stands there, looking puzzled.)

MAMA: I'm sorry... I was trying to...

BOSEDE: Oh, Mama...

KOLA: *(comes inside to join them. He looks annoyed when he sees the broken plate. Bosede leaves them.)* I know you have broken another plates when I heard the sound.

MAMA: I .... I was trying to put it where you normally keep the plates when it fell from my hand.

KOLA: Who told you to touch anything in this house in the first place? There is nothing you touch here that remains the same. Why? I think we've had enough! How could you come into this house and be breaking all our plates!

MAMA: I... I was...

KOLA: I said that's enough! I don't want to hear any more of your excuses. As from now on till you leave this house, I don't want you to touch anything in this house again. And for breaking our plates, you'll be eating with plastic plates from now on.

MAMA: *(signs.)* It's okay.

KOLA: *(goes out.)* Junior! Go and sweep the kitchen. Grandma has broken another plate. *(Mama also leaves the kitchen, looking deeply hurt.)*

SCENE FOUR

(Mama eats on the table with plastic plate. Junior comes out of the room and goes to Mama. He frowns when he sees her eating with plastic plate. He goes to sit in front of her.)

JUNIOR: Mama, why must you eat with plastic plate?

MAMA: Em... That's what... em... your father wants me to use.

JUNIOR: Why? Is it because you broke the plates by mistakes?

MAMA: Yes, child. But don't tell your parents anything. I don't want trouble.

JUNIOR: Grandma, we are taught in my school to always do and say the right thing. I am going to let daddy and mummy know that the way they treat you is bad.

MAMA: *(in a pleading voice.)* Please, don't do anything like that.

73

JUNIOR: Why not?

MAMA: They will think I teach you.

JUNIOR: No, they won't think so. They know Miss Benson, our Bible Club teacher teaches us a lot of moral lessons in the school. There was a time she came here to teach us the right thing to do

MAMA: Please, be careful. I have not come here to cause trouble.

JUNIOR: Don't worry, Grandma. I will pray and God will teach me what to do.

MAMA: Whatever you do or say, just leave me out it. I don't want wahala - problem!

JUNIOR: I would do the right thing for the sake Jesus Christ... *(He goes to put his arm round her)* ... and for you. *(Mama cuddles her.)* I love you...

MAMA: I love you too - very much.

SCENE FIVE

(Junior goes to where the dog is eating and takes the plate and put it inside the nylon bag. Then he goes into the sitting room where Kola and Bosede are talking.)

BOSEDE: Mama seems to be feeling uncomfortable in the house now.

KOLA: Why do you say that?

BOSEDE: She is not as free as when she first came.

KOLA: You should expect that since the time she almost broke all the plates in the house.

BOSEDE: She didn't break them on purpose.

KOLA: She's not an issue for me to discuss. Anyway, I'm thinking of taking her back to her house where she is used to. *(Junior goes to them with the nylon bag. He sits in between them on the couch.)*

BOSEDE: You know interrupting a discussion is not a polite thing to do?

JUNIOR: I'm sorry, mum, but I have something important to show you and daddy.

KOLA: What's it? *(Junior brings the dog's plate out of the bag. He frowns.)* What's this?

BOSEDE: Is that not the plate we normally use to give food to the dog?

JUNIOR: Yes, mummy.

KOLA: Why do you bring it here?

JUNIOR: I want to wash it and keep it for both of you.

BOSEDE: *(looks stunned.)* What for?

JUNIOR: When the two of you get old like grand ma, I won't waste my money to buy breakable plates for you. I'll use this to give you food. *(He stands up, moves closer to the door and points at each of them.)* You will use it together or you will use it one after the other just like the dogs. You don't have to worry about that. I'll teach both of you how to use it when you grow old like Grandma.

KOLA: *(stands up suddenly with anger.)* You mean you will treat both of us like dogs when we get old?! *(He glances at Bosede who also looks more stunned.)*

JUNIOR: Why are you angry at me, dad? If plastic plate that is meant to serve dog is good enough for Grandma, it's also good for both of you, isn't?

KOLA: *(looks angrier as he exchanges glances with Bosede.)* I can kill this boy! *(He tries to make after Junior who runs out of the house but Bosede holds him back.)*

BOSEDE: The boy was only trying to pass a message to us about Mama. Why not listen and think about it instead of trying to bully him? *(There is a brief silence as Kola thoughtfully and slowly sits down.)* He sees the way we are treating your mother. He doesn't like it. So instead of getting angry at him, let us change the way we treat Mama. If we want him to treat us with respect, then let's treat our parents with respect. Really, I didn't know that using plastic plate to serve Mama food is so disrespectful. I can now see why she is no longer feeling comfortable in the house. *(There is silence.)* Don't you think she deserves our apologies for the way we've been treating her? *(He nods thoughtfully.)* We'll do that when Junior is around.

KOLA: No.

BOSEDE: Why not? It's another way of teaching him to say sorry when you go wrong. *(He looks hesitant before he shakes his head.)*

KOLA: No. I'll talk to him about it later.

SCENE SIX

(Mama comes from the room and goes to the sitting room where Bosede and Kola still conversing.)

MAMA: I heard noises. I hope there is no problem.

BOSEDE: Em..., no, Mama…. Please sit down, Mama. *(She helps her to sit on the couch.)* Actually, we're having a minor problem with Junior.

MAMA: You're having problem with Junior?

KOLA: Yes, Mama... It has to do with the way we're treating you.

BOSEDE: *(goes on her kneels.)* We just want to apologize for the way we are treating you.

MAMA: I wonder what you've done that is bad. After all you take good care of me.

KOLA: *(prostrates.)* I'm sorry, Mama. We've been treating you with disrespect.

MAMA: *(frowns.)* How? And what has this got to do with Junior?

BOSEDE: Mama, there's no point trying to explain. The most important thing is that Junior makes us realized that we've been treating you with disrespect. He promised to treat us the same way when we get old. Please, Mama, forgive us. There would be a change

MAMA: *(sighs and shakes her head with wonder.)* Please, sit down. *(She*

75

sits opposite them.) I forgive you from the button of my heart.

KOLA AND BOSEDE: Thank you, Mama.

MAMA: I'm just curious about what Junior did.

BOSEDE: He brought a plastic plate that is meant to serve dog here and told us that he'll keep it for us.

KOLA: He said he'll use it to serve us food when we grow old like you.

MAMA: *(laughs.)* That boy! *(She shakes her head with awe.)* So this is what he planned. I wish you'll appreciate the kind of child God has given you.

KOLA: *(exchanges glances with Bosede before he looks at Mama again.)* You seem to know something about this?

MAMA: He told me he would make you realize that the way you treat me is wrong. I tried to stop him but he had made up his mind.

BOSEDE: I see. Well, I used to thank God for giving him to us. Do you know, Mama, that we tried to get rid of him when I became pregnant of him?

MAMA: What? Why?

BOSEDE: *(looks at Kola.)* Well, Mama, we thought the pregnancy was a mistake.

MAMA: Thank God you didn't get rid of him. Every child either in the womb or not is a gift from God. The gift is for the family, the country and the world.

BOSEDE: *(looks at Kola.)* I guess we should be thinking of having more children.

MAMA: I wanted to ask why you didn't have more children.

KOLA: *(gestures at Bosede.)* She is the cause.

BOSEDE: But I have my reasons for not...

MAMA: Whatever could have been your reason?

BOSEDE: He was a drunkard until he seems to change a little.

KOLA: A little?

BOSEDE: You think I don't know you still drink? I know that as long as you move with those impossible friends of yours, the chance for you to change completely is very remote....

SCENE SEVEN

(Junior sits in the room reading Foundation Story Book. Kola comes to join him. He tries to run from him but when he smiles at him, he relaxes.)

KOLA: Why are you trying to run from me?

JUNIOR: I know I've done something wrong. I'm sorry, daddy.

KOLA: It's okay, son. Let me have a look at the book you're reading. *(Junior gives it to him. He studies the book cover and frowns.)* Is this part of your text books in the school?

JUNIOR: No, dad.

KOLA: But you bought it in the school.

76

JUNIOR: Yes, sir. Mum bought it for me in the school. Miss Benson uses it to teach us Christian Moral Instruction at the Bible Club Fellowship.

KOLA: I know Miss Benson. She is the Christian teacher in your school. *(He opens the book and reads.)* Prayer Is The Key. *(He looks at him.)* This is interesting. *(He continues reading the book, looking at him occasionally. He goes to sit down and continues reading. He nods his head thoughtfully.)* Now I know where you learn the way you are acting.

JUNIOR: Dad, we are not taught to be rude to our parents.

KOLA: I never say you're rude, did I? Actually, you're doing the right thing. You know, it's good to correct parents when they are doing wrong thing. After all what you said to us is for the sake of your Grandma and for our own good.

JUNIOR: How do you know I did it for Grandma?

KOLA: Well, she told us when we apologized to her after getting the lesson you're trying to teach us. I just want to tell you that we won't treat your Grandma with disrespect again so that you don't have to treat us like dogs when we grow old like her.

JUNIOR: I don't really mean to treat you like that when you grow old because I don't my child to treat me like that too.

KOLA: I know, son. *(He beckons on him. Junior sits beside.)* I know you're a good boy. Like me ask you now. Who would you like to be like?

JUNIOR: I like to be like Jesus.

KOLA: Good - good boy!

EPISODE TEN
ENEMIES IN THE HOUSE
SCENE ONE

(The members of secret cult are holding a meeting at the strong room with Olori Awo making incitations.)

OLORI AWO: ...If we say we'll take today, it is tomorrow we will take. Because tomorrow never comes, we can never take any day. "It will descend. It will descend," is how it seems until the butterfly disappears into the bush. Anyone that attempts to consume the child of the grand demon will end up in the belly of the grand demon... What do we have here? *(He looks round at the rest of cult members. He points at one after the other, addressing each of them.)* Do you have your child among the potential successor of members of the Brotherhood Caucus called the Arole?

ADEYORI: *(bows)* My son, Gbenga is among the Arole, my lord.

OLORI AWO: Very good. I remember the time we initiated the boy. Tell me, how is your Arole doing?

ADEYORI: *(smiles proudly.)* He is doing fine. He can now go on an abstract projection.

OLORI AWO: *(nods.)* That's very impressive. *(He points at Deroye.)* How about you?

DEROYE: My Arole is doing fine. *(Olori Awo points at one after the other, including Nuru. Each of them nods with smiles until it is the turn of Kola who looked reluctant.)*

OLORI AWO: *(walks slowly toward him.)* Kola, do you have Arole with us?

KOLA: My lord, you know I have only one child. He's a boy of ten years old.

OLORI AWO: So? *(There is a silence. He points at one of the members.)* Fayomo brought his Arole when the boy was just two years old. (He looks deep into his face.)* So what is your problem with your *ten* year old child?

KOLA: I feel he is too young to be made Arole. Apart from that, his mother had programmed his brain with Church stuff.

OLORI AWO: That's because you didn't take appropriate step when he was born. Besides that, it doesn't look as if you're ready to make the boy your successor when you die.

KOLA: That's not true, my lord. It's the mother that's causing the problem. She continues to say the boy had been covenanted and destined to be a pastor by God when he grows up.

OLOR AWO: *(looks angry.)* Did you hear yourself? What would make your wife say a thing like that if you're not a weak husband?

78

KOLA: I'm sorry. I have no excuse.

OLORI AWO: Then you bring the boy here in the next meeting. We'll first undo whatever had been done to program his brain by making him to bow down to the image of the grand master. Then we'll come to your house to do the final initiation. Is that understood?

KOLA: Yes, my lord. *(Soon Olori Awo begins to make more incarnations.)*

SCENE TWO

(Bosede makes the table in the dinning room as Junior reads the Foundation Bible Club Story Book in the sitting room.)

BOSEDE: Junior!

JUNIOR: *(without looking at her.)* Yes, mum.

BOSEDE: Your food is ready.

JUNIOR: I want to finish reading the story in this book.

BOSEDE: *(goes to join him.)* The food will get cold before you finish reading the story.

JUNIOR: I'll eat it like that.

BOSEDE: *(goes to snatch the book from him.)* Nop! *(She points to the dinning table. He shrugs and goes to the dinning room. She follows him, looking at the book.)* You use the book at the Bible Club Fellowship, don't you?

JUNIOR: *(goes to sit on the dinning chair.)* Yes.

BOSEDE: You are not supposed to read only the story.

JUNIOR: Yes. I read the poems and the sing the song too. *(He pauses for a while to pray silently over the food before he begins to eat it.)*

BOSEDE: *(makes her way to the room, holding the book.)* When you finish your food, you can take the plates to the kitchen and wash them.

JUNIOR: Can I have the book?

BOSEDE: You can come and get it in the room when you finish everything you're supposed to do. *(She goes to the room.)*

SCENE THREE

(Kola enters the sitting room while Junior is still eating at the dinning room. He looks round and sees him.)

JUNIOR: *(sees him.)* Welcome, daddy.

KOLA: *(smiles broadly and goes to join him, putting down his briefcases.)* Hey, Junior, my boy. *(He takes part of his food.)* Oh, yummy! *(He sits beside him.)* Mummy cooked this, isn't it?

JUNIOR: Yes.

KOLA: She is always a great cook! Where is she?

JUNIOR: She's gone inside the room.

KOLA: I have something to tell you. Promise me you won't tell her.

JUNIOR: What is it?

79

KOLA: You need to first promise me you won't tell her.

JUNIOR: Okay.

KOLA: You know promise is a debt. If you don't keep your promise, God can take you to hell.

AYAFE: I won't tell her.

KOLA: Good! I'll take you out to a meeting with some of my friends. We are going to do some things there. Then we'll take delicious food like fried plantain and chicken with baked beans and boiled egg.

JUNIOR: Wao!

KOLA: Yeah! I know you love food. Would you go with me?

JUNIOR: Yes, of course. When?

KOLA: When it is time, I will tell you. It's going to be late in the night because it's a night party.

JUNIOR: *(frowns.)* What's night party?

KOLA: On, it's... em... party at night.

JUNIOR: But we are taught at the Bible Club Fellowship in the school that that kind of party it's not... em. . . in line with the Bible.

KOLA: Never mind what they tell you in the school.

JUNIOR: Can mummy follow us?

KOLA: No. I told you I don't want her to know about it.

JUNIOR: *(shrugs.)* Okay.

KOLA: That's my boy.

SCENE FOUR

(Junior is among the students in the class, listening to the Miss Benson who holds a Bible and he story book.)

MISS BENSON: You're welcome to today's Bible Club Fellowship. *(She raises the book up for everybody to see.)* I hope everybody is having a copy of this book.

STUDENTS: Yes, Ma.

MISS BENSON: Who can tell us the title of the story we studied last week? *(Most of the students raise of their hands.)* Segun, you can tell us.

SEGUN: *(stands up.)* The Idol Town.

MISS BENSON: Good. Which passage of the Bible did we read? *(Again some students raise their hands up.)* Sola can tell us.

SOLA: We read the book of Psalm chapter one hundred and sixteen verses four to eight.

MISS BENSON: Good. I want everybody to recite the passage in verses seven and eight which I told you memorize. One . . . two. Go!

STUDENTS: Return unto your rest, O my soul; for the LORD had dealt bountifully with you. For You have delivered my soul from death, my eyes from tears, and my feet from falling.

MISS BENSON: That's very good. You can recite the rhyme about the idol

80

together.

STUDENTS: *I is for Idol*
That looks so dull
It is taken as a god
But we know it is a doll
And not the real God

MISS BENSON: Good. Before we go into today's story titled: Sheep In The Jungle, let's sing the song about idol.

STUDENTS: *What connection do we have with idols*
Which cannot deliver from sin?
We won't have anything to do with them
We are secured in Jesus Christ
I wonder what people see in idols
We must show the real way
For they don't know the way to heaven
The Lord will give the grace.

MISS BENSON: *(smiles at them.)* Now give yourself big round of applause. *(The students clap their hands with joy.)* Before we start today's lesson, who will lead up in prayer?

JUNIOR: *(quickly raises up his hand.)* Junior, lead us in prayer.

JUNIOR: Father we thank you for today...

SCENE FIVE

(Kola appears to have slept beside Bosede. After a moment, he opens his eyes and looks at her briefly. He gets up slowly and silently. He gets out of the room and goes to Junior's room. Junior is sound asleep. He taps him silently. Junior wakes up, looking startled when he sees him.)

KOLA: It's time to go.

JUNIOR: *(looks confused.)* Where?

KOLA: Sssh! *(He looks behind him.)* Keep your voice down. You'll wake up your mum. We are going to the place I told you about the other time.

JUNIOR: You mean the party?

KOLA: Yes.

JUNIOR: I want to sleep. I don't want to go to anywhere now.

KOLA: Come on, get up. *(He pulls him.)* We are going now.

JUNIOR: Okay, okay. Shall we pray first?

KOLA: You can pray but keep your voice down.

JUNIOR: *(kneel down and begin to pray.)* Dear lord, we thank you...

SCENE SIX

(The members of the cult gather in the strong room with Olori Awo, making chant. After a while, Kola enters with Junior who looks reluctant to enter.)

OLORI AWO: Kola. You and your son are late.

81

KOLA: I am sorry, my lord. We had a delay on our way here.

OLORI AWO: We'll come to that later. *(He looks at Junior who looks round with confusion.)* Is this the boy that is supposed to be your Arole?

KOLA: *(looks at Junior.)* Yes, my lord.

JUNIOR: *(looks at Kola.)* Daddy, what are we doing here?

KOLA: You be a good boy and keep your mouth shut.

OLORI AWO: *(moves closer to Kola.)* You obviously didn't tell the boy your mission here, did you?

KOLA: Yes, I couldn't. As I told you, he's been programmed by his mother not to follow anything that is contrary to the Bible.

OLORI AWO: We'll look into that. *(He beckons on Junior to come to him, moving towards him.)* Come here, boy. *(Junior goes to Kola and holds his hand.)*

KOLA: *(looks at him.)* Come on, go to him. He won't hurt.

JUNIOR: No, daddy. I don't want him to touch me. Let's go home. I don't like this place.

KOLA: We'll go home when we finish what we've come here to do.

JUNIOR: No, Daddy! Please, let's go home.

OLORI AWO: *(glares at Kola.)* I am going to hurt the boy or even shed his blood if he doesn't cooperate with us.

JUNIOR: *(looks frightened.)* Daddy, w-why d-did y-you bring me here?

KOLA: It's for your own good, son. Trust me. Come on, go to him. *(He takes his hand and gently leads him to Olori Awo.)*

OLORI AWO: *(points at an image among the fetish items in the room.)* Go and kneel down in front of the master of the universe. *(Junior looks at Kola with more confused expression.)* If you refuse to do that, I'll kill you with my bare hands.

JUNIOR: God says we should not bow down to any idol. *(Olori Awo looks angrily at Kola.)*

OLORI AWO: Did he just call the master of the universe an idol?

KOLA: Calm down, my lord. I'll talk to the boy. He is not used to this place.

OLORI AWO: My patience is running thin! If a boy of just ten years would give us a problem of this size, you can be sure he can become too monstrous for us to tame if he grows older. If you want this boy to leave this place alive, tell him to bow to the master of the universe.

KOLA: *(takes Junior's hand and leads him to the image, facing it together.)* You will do as I do if you don't want to die. I don't want you to die. You know your mummy would kill herself if you die. *(Junior looks more frightened.)* Do you want to die?

JUNIOR: *(shakes his head quickly, looking frightened.)* Please, daddy, let us go back home. This place is...

OLORI AWO: If you don't do what you're told, you're going nowhere!

KOLA: *(pulls and forces Junior to prostrate as he bows in front of the image. He also prostrates.)* My son and I worship you, the master of the universe.

OLORI AWO: We have to do the ritual and initiation in your house next week.

KOLA: What?

OLORI AWO: Do you have problem with that?

KOLA: Not really, my lord but...

OLORI AWO: But me no buts. If we procrastinate, we risk we'll risk losing the boy. As I said, if he can give us so much trouble now, you can be sure, he can pose much more threats later. Besides, the boy now knows too much about us. So we'll not waste time initiating him immediately. We'll get ready all items of initiations before then. Do you understand? *(Kola nods reluctantly.)* You can go and keep the boy in the waiting room while we tend to other things. *(Kola leads Junior out of the strong room.)*

SCENE SEVEN

(Kola and Junior come into Junior's room. Junior goes to sit down silently on bed, looking downcast.)

KOLA: You're still angry at me. *(There is silence the sits beside him.)* I'm sorry, son.

JUNIOR: You made me sin against God.

KOLA: Oh, no. You've not sinned against God.

JUNIOR: We were taught in the church and in the Bible Club Fellowship not to believe in any one except Jesus. You made me bow down to idol. *(He begins to cry, covering his face.)*

KOLA: Ssh... You'll wake your mother up.

JUNIOR: I don't care!

KOLA: I'll beat the shit out of you if she wakes up.

JUNIOR: Then I'll tell her what happened.

KOLA: *(stands up suddenly. looking angry.)* Are you threatening me?

JUNIOR: We've been told to always tell the truth. So I'm going to tell her.

KOLA: *(slaps him across the face. Junior cries with pain.)* Shut up. *(He mutters. He shows him his fist.)* If you make a sound, I will hit you on the face. *(Junior covers his mouth, trying not to suppress the sound of his cries.)* If you tell your mother, I'll tell the men to take you away when you are sleeping at night. *(Junior looks horrified.)* Would you tell her?

JUNIOR: *(still suppressing the sobs, shaking his head vigorously.)* I won't!

KOLA: *(pulls him to himself.)* I'm sorry. You're the one making me do this to you. You know I love you. I'll buy something you like tomorrow. What do you want me to buy for you?

JUNIOR: I d-don't want anything.

KOLA: You're still angry at me? Don't worry. I'll make you happy. You can go to sleep now. I'll do something that would make you happy later.

JUNIOR: I want talk to God first.

KOLA: If it'll make you happy, you can talk to him. I'll see you later. *(He goes out of the room. Junior kneels beside the bed.)*

JUNIOR: *(begins to sobs.)* Dear Lord Jesus, I am sorry for what I did today. My father made me bow down before an idol. Please, forgive me and help me to fight anyone who wants to take me away from you in Jesus' name. Amen. *(He lies on his bed, drying the tears on his face. A moment later, he sleeps. As he sleeps, he dreams that an old comes into the same room. Old man goes to sit beside him on the bed, smiling at him. He touches the tears on his eyes while he is still sleeping.)*

OLD MAN: Junior, My child. *(Junior opens his eyes in the dream. Old man smiles at him and touches his laps.)* Come and sit here. *(Junior goes to sit on his laps.)* Even though you cannot see me. I am with you. I will never leave you. Even though your mother or anyone cannot fight for you, I will fight for you.

JUNIOR: Who are you?

OLD MAN: I'm your Father from heaven.

JUNIOR: You mean Jesus?

OLD MAN: *(smiles.)* Yes.

JUNIOR: But I see different pictures about you. Which one is real you, Father?

OLD MAN: You have a very curious mind, son. I do appear to people in different ways but it is the same me. Sometimes I send angels to my people but I have to come to you by Myself because you need Me

JUNIOR: *(cuddles him.)* Wao! Thank you so much, Father.

OLD MAN: I love you so much.

JUNIOR: I love too.

OLD MAN: You're the apple of my eyes, son. Anyone that fights you fights Me. I will never allow anyone to do you any harm. I will put all your enemies into shame when they come to you. Then you father will know that you have a Father in heaven who fights fro you. Don't cry again and don't be afraid of any of them. I will fight for you. Do you understand? *(Junior nods with smiles.)* Sleep well because you're save in My hands. *(The scene changes to Junior still sleeping on the bed, an indication that the dream looks real. Bosede comes into the room, singing.)*

BOSEDE: *I have seen Jesus*
            I have seen Jesus
            He's more handsome than any man....

(She goes to sit beside him.) Junior, sleeping beauty. Waky! Waky! It's getting late and you have not said your prayers yet. *(He wakes up with a start.)* It's time for prayers. *(Junior sit son the bed with a yawn.)*

JUNIOR: Good morning, mum.

BOSEDE: I told you to always say good morning to Jesus first before saying good morning to anyone. He's been keeping watch over you since. He never sleeps nor slumbers because of you.

JUNIOR: *(looks surprised.)* How do you know that?

BOSEDE: How do I know what?

JUNIOR: How do you know Jesus keeps watch over me?

BOSEDE: I expect you to have come across the lesson about God's protection in your Story Book. Besides, the word of God says so in Psalm 121 verse 4. *(She takes and opens the Bible beside his bed.)* It says, Behold, he that keeps Israel… *(She looks at him.)* If you replace Israel in the passage with your name, it 'll read, *"He that keep Junior shall neither slumber nor sleep."* *(She looks at her as he nods with smiles.)*

JUNIOR: An old man came to me in the dream and told me He is with me. He sat down where you sit and put me on his laps. He said that I am the apple of his eyes.

BOSEDE: That proves you're true child of God. The old man is Jesus.

JUNIOR: I know, mum.

BOSEDE: No wonder the Spirit of God makes me sing the song about seeing Jesus this morning.

JUNIOR: *(looks excited.)* Really?

BOSEDE: Yes! *(She begins to sing again.)* I have seen Jesus... *(Junior sings with her. After a while, the song ceases.)* Now let's do the morning prayers. *(She leads him in prayers.)*

EPISODE ELEVEN
ENEMIES WITHIN AND WITHOUT
SCENE ONE

(Olori Awo is in the strong room, making incantation when Kola claps three times before he enters.)

OLORI AWO: You're welcome, son of the grand master.

KOLA: Thank you, my lord. I hope all is well.

OLORI AWO: All is well. I sent for you because of the issue of initiation of your son. With what happened that day, it occurs to me that your son has a stubborn spirit. So we have to prepare extra ritual materials that would assure us that he is successfully initiated. If we don't, he is may give us problem. You will have to go to Awo Agbede river to get the water which would be part of what we will use to initiate the boy.

KOLA: *(looks confused.)* Can't we get someone to do that for us? I'm ready to pay the person.

OLORI AWO: You're the only one who can do that unless he has two fathers.

KOLA: *(looks thoughtful for a while.)* When do you want me to do that?

OLORI AWO: I need to invoke some spirits into the water tonight. So it is better you go and get it now.

KOLA: I didn't prepare for this!

OLORI AWO: You don't need to prepare for anything before you get me the water from the river. All you need now is a specially prepared calabash which you'll use to fetch it.

KOLA: *(shrugs after a brief hesitation.)* Okay. Where is ths calabash?

OLORI AWO: I'll get it for you now.

SCENE TWO

(Junior is doing his home work in the sitting room when Bosede comes out of the room. She hesitates for a while before she goes to sit beside him.)

BOSEDE: Are you just doing your assignment?

JUNIOR: Yes. *(He looks at her as she turns to leave.)* Mum... *(She turns back to look at him.)* There is a song I cannot sing very well in my story book. I wonder if you can help me with the song. We are to sing the song on Friday.

BOSEDE: There is time for everything. You can't do two things at a time and you can mist up academic works with Bible Club Bible assignments. You can do your school assignment first.

JUNIOR: I've almost finish the school assignment. I need you to help me with the song. I'll complete assignment when you teach me the song.

BOSEDE: You can complete the school assignment first. I'll teach you the song later.

JUNIOR: Please, mum. I don't want daddy to come and disturb us when practicing the song.

BOSEDE: Okay. *(She goes to sit beside him. He brings out the Foundation Bible Club Story Book in his bag. He opens it and shows her the page.)*

JUNIOR: This is the song.

BOSEDE: You don't known the tune?

JUNIOR: *(shakes his head.)* No.

BOSEDE: Here... *(She points at a place in the book.)* You are to use the tune of the song titled: "From East To East" to sing it.

JUNIOR: I don't know the song.

BOSEDE: It goes like this: *(She clears her throat to sing.)*

> *From east to west*
> *I say there's no other God*
> *From north to south*
> *I say there's no other*

When you know the tune of that song. You can sing the one here like this:

> *From day till night*
> *I know God is by my side*
> *From night till day*
> *I know God will never leave me.*

Now let's sing it together. (Junior looks at the book.) We'll sing the original song before we sing the one in the book, okay? (He nods with smiles. They begin to sing together.)

> *From east to west*
> *I say there's no other God...*

SCENE THREE

(Kola holds nylon bag in his hand, going toward the river. After walking for a while, getting close to the river, he brings out a calabash from the bag. He walks into the river to get some water. As he gets out of the river with the calabash in his hand, ready to go home, a mad man starts singing, dancing and coming his way. He stops beside Kola and smiles at him.)

MAD MAN: Hello, my friend! *(Kola smiles, waves at him and start going.)* Hay, that's not how to greet a friend. Give me some water to drink.

KOLA: *(points at the river.)* You can get all you need there.

MAD MAN: What am I supposed to fetch it with, you dummy?

KOLA: Go inside, put your mouth inside and drink all you want.

MAD MAN: You want me to get drowned?

KOLA: Who cares if you're drowned? *(He begins to leave.)*

MAD MAN: Come back here, you, wicked man! *(He runs after him and struggles to take the calabash from him until it breaks. Kola looks so angry that he begins to fight the mad man.)*

KOLA: I'll kill you today and feed the fishes in the river with your body. *(They begin to fight until the mad man beat and wounds him. Kola later takes to his heel, running as fast as he can. The mad man runs after him.)*

MAD MAN: Wait for me and let me teach you how to be polite to elders!

SCENE FOUR

(Olori Awo is still in strong room, making incantation when Kola comes inside. He is looks very tired and wounded.)

OLORI AWO: *(looks agitated.)* What's wrong?

KOLA: I told you I'm not prepared for this but you don't believe me. The worst has happened. *(He brings out the broken calabash.)* I met a mad man who beat me so much that I cannot remember much of what happened. The only thing I remember is that he broke the calabash after beating the hell out of me.

OLORI AWO: *(looks thoughtful for a while, nodding.)* This is interesting....

KOLA: Do you know what is going on?

OLORI AWO: *(sighs.)* Your son already belongs to a cult - a powerful cult for that matter. I wonder at the kind of cult that would admit child of your son's age.

KOLA: *(waves impatiently.)* Oh, no. My son doesn't belong to any cult. I am sure of that.

OLORI AWO: What makes you so sure?

KOLA: We are talking about my son here. I know virtually everything about him.

OLORI AWO: No, you don't. The mad man you met is a spirit that was sent by the head of the cult which your child belongs to.

KOLA: You may be right about the mad man, going by his strength but I'm sure the child does not belong to any cult. The boy's school teacher and mother influence him to believe so much in God that he cannot believe in any other thing. Unless you want to say his belief in God is what makes him a cult member.

OLORI AWO: Let's not drag the issue unnecessarily. What happened is a proof that initiating the boy would be a tug of war. We are not going to use water as we planned. We'll use blood.

KOLA: *(looks surprised.)* What? He's a young boy, not an adult. We are not initiating him into the cult yet, are we?

OLORI AWO: If the boy or whoever is acting on his behalf is strong enough to sent a mad man to contend with us, we need stronger item to get him to

88

cooperate with us. You were here when he almost refused to bow to the grand master.

KOLA: How are we going to make him drink blood? Whose blood anyway?

OLORI AWO: The blood of he-goat - a stubborn goat. You're going to buy it.

KOLA: Okay, okay. But that has not really answer the question of how to make him drink it.

OLORI AWO: Leave that to me. *(Kola looks suspicious.)* If you think I'm going to force or threaten him, you're wrong. He's going to drink it willingly after a few incantations.

KOLA: *(looks thoughtful and then nods.)* Okay. I hope it works.

OLORI AWO: I can assure you it'll work. The method had never failed.

KOLA: When do we perform the initiation?

OLORI AWO: It has be tomorrow.

KOLA: Don't you think that's so soon?

OLORI AWO: Procrastination is the thief of time. The more we delay, the more we give the boy the chance to grow out of hand. It's because you delayed the initiation that made the boy to grow wings in the first place. So tomorrow we'll assemble in your house. You have to find a way to get rid of your wife before we get to the house.

SCENE FIVE

(Bosede and Junior are in the sitting room. She teaches him some things in the Bible)

BOSEDE: ...That passage in the book of Psalm Chapter Ninety-One Verse One and Two says... *(She points it to him in the Bible.)* He who dwells in the secret place of the Most High shall abide under the shadow of the Almighty. I will say of the Lord, He is my refuge and my fortress: My God in Him will I trust.

JUNIOR: *(looks confused.)* What does that mean?

BOSEDE: *(looks curiously at him.)* Since you told me told me about the old man that came to you in the dream, things are different. *(Junior smiles, nodding.)* Well, let me explain it this way. *"He that dwells in the secret place of the Most High shall abide under the shadow of the Almighty"* means that anyone that is always with God shall be under His protection. The next verse means that the person would say to the Lord Jesus, *"You are my refuge and fortress. I will trust in you."*

JUNIOR: What's the meaning of refuge and fortress?

BOSEDE: Refuge and fortress mean almost the same. Both means shelter or a building like a house.

JUNIOR: *(looks confused.)* You mean Jesus is like a house?

BOSEDE: We can say yes because we live inside Jesus and Jesus live inside us.

JUNIOR: *(looks exited.)* Wao! You mean that old man - Jesus lives inside me?

89

BOSEDE: *(smiles at him.)* Yes, of course. Let's see it in First book of John Chapter Four Verse Four. *(She opens the passage in the Bible.)* You can memorize it so that you will always remember that Jesus lives inside you. You can read the place by yourself.

JUNIOR: *(takes the Bible and begins to read it.)* "You are of God, little children, and have overcome them; because He who is in you is greater than he that is in the world." *(He looks excitedly at Bosede.)* Wao! *(Bosede keeps smiling at him.)* I will never be afraid again.

BOSEDE: Were you afraid before now?

JUNIOR: Yes.

BOSEDE: What were you afraid of?

JUNIOR: I don't want to tell you that.

BOSEDE: Okay but you have to know what the Bible says about fear in Second Timothy Chapter One Verse Seven. *(She takes the Bible from him again, opens and gives it to him.)* You can read the passage there.

JUNIOR: *(reads the passage aloud.)* For God has not given us the spirit of fear; but of power, and of love and of sound mind. *(He looks thoughtful.)*

BOSEDE: It's the devil that makes us to be afraid so that we wont be able to use the power of Jesus to defeat him.

JUNIOR: *(looks thoughtful as he recalls the flash back of episode ten scene six.)* Really?

BOSEDE: Yes! Why do you think Miss Benson told you to learn the songs titled: "From Day Till Night" in your story book? If you read the story, you'll see that it teaches you not to be afraid because Jesus is with you.

JUNIOR: Yes! I remember the story. It's about a boy and his sisters that were afraid of the night.

BOSEDE: That's it. Now let's sing the song together. *(They begin to sing the song.)*

     From day till night....

EPISODE TWELVE
THE GREATER POWER
SCENE ONE

(Miss Benson sits with Sade outside the house, talking. Sade looks sorrowful.)

MISS BENSON: *(looks a little confused.)* You mean you and your sister shared the same husband?

SADE: *(in a whisper.)* Yes.

MISS BENSON: Where is she now?

SADE: She's dead now - after placing a curse on me and the family. You're the second person I'll share this with. The other person I told is Junior's mother who introduced you to me. *(Suddenly, she bursts out sobbing, covering her face with her both palms. After a while, she takes the handkerchief on the table and wipes her tears. Miss Benson is trying to recover from her confusion.)* I've been living in pains, sorrow - mental torture for years. I'm not sure how long I'll last before I bid the world goodbye. I feel it deep inside me that I'm close to my grave. Still, I feel concerned for my children and that of my sister. I want them to know God. *(She begins to sob again.)* I don't want them to grow up and follow my footsteps or that of their father. I think of it over and over, wondering how I can possibly make a U turn but I can't find a way out of the web of total destruction. *(Tears run down her face.)* I desperately need forgiveness of God and the hope of eternity.

MISS BENSON: *(smiles briefly and touches her hand.)* There's hope.

SADE: *(looks at her with depression.)* Hope? Where? I can't see any.

MISS BENSON: *(brings out her Bible in her bags and shows her.)* This is where your hope. If you believe it, you will see it; you will feel it and you will get out of the web of destruction.

SADE: Please, show me. I'm desperate.

MISS BENSON: *(opens the Bible.)* The word of God tells us in Isaiah Chapter 64 Verse 6 that we are all like unclean thing but He assured us in the same book Chapter 1 verse 18 that though we are made like scarlet by sins and red like crimson, we shall be made as white as snow. God also makes us to understand in First Book of Peter Chapter 1 verse 25 that we like sheep that have gone astray but the mysterious thing about God is that He never hold our sins against us, no matter how great they are because He is mindful of the fact that we are ordinary clay. People might have condemned you but God never condemn anyone, at least not before the person departs from this world. Take for instance the story of the woman that was brought to Jesus in the Gospel according to Saint John chapter 8 verses 3 to 11. The scribes and Pharisees who were full of holier-than-thou

91

attitude accused the woman of committing adultery. They expected Jesus to condemn her on the spot. There was miscarriage of justice right from the onset. Firstly, it takes two people to commit adultery but only one person was brought. Secondly, they were not in the position to judge anyone because they were also sinners. Jesus pointed this out to them by saying that anyone without a sin should cast the first stone. They left the woman alone. The reason they have to leave her is because they will all be dead if they are to be judged as they judged the woman.

Obviously, you're thinking you have crossed the borderline of mercy by sharing your sister's husband but the truth is: you have not. No one has ever crossed the borderline of mercy, no matter what they have done. The sins we commit don't really offend God as much as we think but what actually makes Him angry is what we do after we realize that we have committed sin. You are not going through this torture because your sister cursed you. You are going through this because of what the Word of God says in Isaiah Chapter 59 verses 1 to 12. If you study the passage very well, you will see that sins separate people so far away from God that it looks as if He cannot reach or hear them. In verses 7 and 8, we understand that sinners run from one evil to another, walking on the path of wasting and destructions. They never find the way of peace because of their sins that keep fishing them out. But Jesus, through His death on the cross, reconciles us with God. As the Gospel according to Saint John Chapter 1 verse 12 says, as many as receive Jesus into their lives, they are given power to become the children of God. It is after you have Jesus in your life that you can really be at peace with God. As you know, the greatest blessing in life is to be at peace with your Maker.

Now that you have realized your mistake, what you do now will determine what God will do to you - pardon you or destroy you in hell when you die.

SADE: How do I get God's pardon?

MISS BENSON: That's a very good question but with simple answer. Give your life to Jesus right now and make right the wrongs you have done.

SADE: How do I make right the wrong?

MISS BENSON: When we pray now after you have given your life to Jesus, you'll have to leave the man you are living with because he is definitely not your husband. *(Sade looks puzzled.)* Is it hard for you to do?

SADE: Oh, no? I'm thinking of the consequences.

MISS BENSON: *(smiles.)* We use to teach children a poem which goes like this. There is fire on the mountain! Run! Run! Run! *(Sade leans backward on the chair, wrapped in deep thoughts.)*

SCENE TWO
(Kola, Junior and Bosede are sitting at the dinning table; eating. Kola absent mindedly stares at the food. Bosede looks at him across the table.)
BOSEDE: What's the matter, honey? You've been so moody for days now.

92

KOLA: *(looks at her and at Junior who also looks at him.)* I have a confession to make.

BOSEDE: Really? What is it about?

KOLA: I was lured into a secret cult shortly after Junior was born.

BOSEDE: Secret cult? *(She looks at Junior briefly.)* Are you sure Junior should hear this?

KOLA: *(snorts.)* He played a major role in what happened to me.

BOSEDE: What? *(She looks puzzled. Junior smiles at her.)* What happened?

JUNIOR: *(looks at Kola.)* There is no need to say anything, dad. Everything is over. All you need to do is to do as we agreed.

BOSEDE: *(looks more confused.)* What exactly is happening here?

KOLA: *(looks thoughtful as he reflects and narrates the events in flashbacks.)* I was told to present Junior at the cult as the one that would succeed me when I die. I told the head of the cult that you have given him to Jesus as a covenant child but he would not believe me. He insisted that I must present him to be reprogrammed. Against my wish, I deceived Junior into going to the place. He was told to bow to the idol which I forced him to do...

JUNIOR: *(looks at Bosede.)* That was before the old man I told you about came to me in the dream.

BOSEDE: *(looks excited.)* I see!

KOLA: The cult head discovered that he's not an ordinary child. He, therefore, told me to get some water at Awo Agbede river but a mad man stopped me. Since I've been told to get rid of you before the day Junior would be initiated in the house... *(He stares at Bosede.)* I have to tell you to take some items to Mama in the village so that you'll not be around. *(He pauses to take a deep breath.)* At the appointed time, the cult members came to this house to initiate Junior as Arole. *(He looks thoughtful as he recalls the incidents in Flashbacks.)*

SCENE THREE
(FLASHBACK)

(Junior reads the Bible in his room .He stands up after a while and begins to pray. Then he goes to lie on the bed to sleep. After a while, Kola comes inside to wake him up.)

KOLA: Junior, Junior... *(Junior wakes up.)* My friends have come to see you.

JUNIOR: Who...?

KOLA: My friends.

JUNIOR: They are evil men...

KOLA: *(glowers at him.)* How dare you call my friends evil!

JUNIOR: Dad, they are not supposed to be your friends. We've been taught not to make friends with vultures because we are doves. We are different

93

people, dad!

KOLA: Young man, don't make me angry now. You've given me enough problems. So get up and come and meet them now!

JUNIOR: I don't want to meet them. *(Kola grabs him from the bed, looking furious.)* Dad, don't think God will allow you do whatever you like to me.

KOLA: Oh, yes I can do whatever I like to you because I'm your father!

JUNIOR: Jesus is my real Father. *(Kola pulls him to the sitting where the cult members are waiting.)*

OLORI AWO: *(smiles at Junior as Kola pushes him to the center of the cult members.)* Son, don't give us headache this time.

JUNIOR: I am not your son! There is nothing you 'll do that will make me part of you because you all evil!

KOLA: *(looks so stunned that he gapes at him.)* What?!

OLORI AWO: *(looks at him.)* Calm down. Actually I expect him to give us problem but you don't have to worry about that. We are prepared for him. *(He moves closer to Junior.)* We can do this in an easy way or hard way. *(He stretches his hand at one of the cult members who hands him a calabash of water. He stretches at Junior.)* Take and drink this now... That's the easy way. The hard way. *(He stretches his hand to the member again. He is given a long dagger. He points it at Junior.)* That's one of the hard ways. *(He gives the dagger back to the member and takes a fetish looking horn of a goat from under his cap. He shows it to Junior.)* If I use this to strike you on the head, you will turn into imbecile. Do you know who is called imbecile?

JUNIOR: No but I don't care.

OLORI AWO: You better care because if I turn you into an imbecile, you'll be as dumb as a sheep. *(Junior looks thoughtful for a while.)* Now tell me which method you want me to use. *(He stretches the calabash to him again.)* Do you want to take the easy way and drink this or you want me to kill you with the dagger or turn your brain into the brain of a sheep by hitting you with my power?

JUNIOR: I will never drink it. Do whatever you want. I know God will save me from you. The book of Psalm chapter 23 says: the Lord is my Shepherd. I shall not want. He makes me lie down in green pasture. He leads me beside the still waters. He restores my soul; He leads me in the paths of righteousness for His name's sake. Even though I walk through the valley of shadow of death, I will fear no evil...

KOLA: *(hurries to him.)* You better shut up there and drink the water!

JUNIOR: I won't!

OLORI AWO: *(flares up with fury and frustrations.)* Then I will turn you into a mad boy!

KOLA: *(appealing to him.)* Please, Olori Awo, don't do that. He's just a boy.

OLORI AWO: *(glares at him.)* You call him a boy? This is not a boy! No one - not even an adult gives us so much trouble in the history of the

Brotherhood! And you are the cause of all these mess! If you have brought him to us when he was younger, we don't have to go through this pain. With the problem he has given us so far, he's already a man! You can be sure we'll treat him like a great enemy if he does cooperate with us now!

KOLA: I'll talk to him.

JUNIOR: Dad, don't border talking to me about it. I'm not going to give myself to anyone except Jesus. I know God will protect me from them. The Bible says greater is God is in me than what is in the world. God also said that no weapon form against me shall prosper. If they don't leave this house, I will command fire from heaven to destroy you now. If you think I can't, try me! *(All the cult members, including Kola look stunned. Suddenly Olori Awo hits Junior on the head with the charm. Instead of feeling pains, Junior begins to sing, dancing round the men.)*

JUNIOR: *God of Elijah sends down fire!*
             God of Elijah sends down fire!

(There is commotion in the house as it appears as if all the men can perceive heat in the house. Junior continues to sing, making all of them to feel heat the more.)

             The God that answers by fire
             Let Him be my God!

OLORI AWO: *(screams at Junior.)* Stop the fire now!

JUNIOR: I won't unless you get out of here! *(He continues singing. Kola falls down on the couch while get the rest of the men find their way out of the house as quickly as their stamina can permit them. After they leave, Junior goes to the door.)* Don't ever come here again if you don't want to die! *(He closes and locks the door before he goes to Kola.)* Dad, don't die yet. You're still going to pay my school fees.

KOLA: *(in a weak voice.)* You really think this funny?

JUNIOR: Well, dad, I've got good and bad news for you. You have to pick the one you want. The good news is that God loves you so much that He sent Jesus to die for you. So I want you to be born-again and leave the cult. If you don't, the bad news is for you. The bad news is that the fire will continue to burn you until you die. I don't want you to die and go to hell. So I want you to become born-again. What do you say?

KOLA: *(in a quiet voice.)* I... don't know. Let me... think about it.... But pray for me now.

SCENE TWO CONTINUES

KOLA: *(looks at Bosede.)* Junior used the power of Jesus to tackle everyone of us in the cult, including the head of the cult. What is even more surprising is the decision of the cult members to expel me without me asking them to let me to leave the Brotherhood. One of them told me that they would have tried to kill me but they fear Junior can tackle them with power he had used to fight them. If Jesus can be so real in life of a boy of his age, then I really need to become born-again.

95

BOSEDE: Praise God! *(She stands up excitedly, going on her kneels, singing.)*

> We are serving a God of miracle,
> I know, yes, I know....
> We have a God who never fails....
> Amen, Jesus never fails....

(The rest joins her in praising God, kneeling down in adoration.)

SCENE FOUR

(Sade comes out of the compound with her luggage as the children follow her looking unhappy.)

FOLA: Mummy, where are you traveling to?

SADE: I'm not traveling. I just want to pack out of the house.

YEMI: Why, mum?

SADE: You can't understand if I tell you.

GIFT: Are you going to leave us behind?

SADE: I've told you when your dad comes, we shall discuss where you will stay.

FOLA: Who is going to take care of us?

SADE: You're big enough to look after your brothers and sisters. When your father comes, I'll call him on the phone and tell him what is happening.

FOLA: Tell us what's happening, mum.

SADE: *(controls her emotions.)* It is never my wish to leave you but I have to under the circumstances I find myself.

FOLA: You've not explained what is happening, mum.

SADE: I can't say more, I'm sorry. *(She begins to leave.)*

FOLA: That's not fair, mummy! Is it because your sister is my real mum that makes you unfair to me?

SADE: *(pauses briefly, looking stunned. She looks back at him with a frown.)* Who told you that?

FOLA: *(moves closer to her.)* I may be too young to understand, at least, I remember that I have a mother who I know is your sister. *(He goes to hold her gently.)* You didn't treat us differently from your real children. That's the reason we have no reason to talk about our real mother. *(She puts down her luggage and stares more firmly at him.)* If you leave, I understand why. We know you've been through so much pains. Daddy treats you like a slave in the house. We use to cry in the room when he beats you. *(He and the rest of the children begin to sob.)* We talk about how we will help you but there is nothing we can do now. We still need you to look after us until we are old enough to be of help.

SADE: *(beckons and hugs the children all together.)* You're all good children. That's more than enough reason for me to go through the torture and the agony your father subjects me into. But there are other reasons - very power ones that make it impossible for me to stay.

FOLA: What are the reasons, mum?

SADE: *(tries to hide her tears with her palms. She cleans it and then looks at him and whispers.)* I am born- again.

FOLA: But that's not enough reason you should leave us. *(He begins to sobs like the rest of the children.)* We... we still need you....

SADE: I know. As you can see, it's not easy for me carry out this decision. This is what God wants me to do after I become born-again. I have to put right things that I have done wrong. That is the only way I can be at peace with Jesus who saves us from destruction.

FOLA: *(looks confused.)* I don't understand. What are you putting right by leaving us?

SADE: *(hesitates for a while, looking thoughtful again.)* Okay, I'll explain if you promise me you'll forgive me.

FOLA: Of course, I will. We've been taught in the School Fellowship by our Chaplain to always forgive anyone that wrongs us.

SADE: *(smiles.)* That'll make things a little easy for me.

FOLA: *(returns the smiles.)* You were the one that took us to the school, remember?

SADE: Of course, I know. Come... *(She signs and pulls him away from the rest of the children by the hand.)* Fola, your father is not my husband. *(He frowns.)* He's your mother's husband.

FOLA: *(looks confused.)* What?

SADE: Yes. Your mother is my sister, as you know. She didn't approve of any of the men I wanted to marry. When I became sorrowful, your father comforted me and then later took me to bed... *(He looks more confused.)* I'm not sure if this is the kind of thing a teenager should hear... I became pregnant. That is what caused your mother to kill herself. I'm sorry, Fola... *(She begins to cry, looking at his face.)*

FOLA: *(in a quiet voice.)* It's okay, mum. I love you still anyway.

SADE: *(looks surprised amidst her tears.)* You still love me despite that?

FOLA: *(nods vigorously, smiling and stretching his ands at her for a hug.)* Yes. *(She hugs him tightly.)*

SADE: You're going to help me put things right, aren't you?

FOLA: With God on our side, yes.

SADE: First, I don't want you to tell anyone what I just told you.

FOLA: I won't unless I have to.

SADE: What do you mean?

FOLA: I may have to tell others if I have to defend your action. Besides, we can't hide it for so long.

SADE: *(smiles, touching his cheek tenderly.)* You're right. The next thing I want you to do for me is to take care of your brothers and sisters. I'm counting on you to do that. Would you do that for me?

FOLA: Sure, mum.

SADE: *(smiles.)* Thank you. Please, convince the children that I love them and I'll be in touch with you through my friend, Mama Junior or Miss Benson. I'm sure you're familiar with them, aren't you

FOLA: Of course, I am. But, please, don't keep us waiting for so long.

SADE: I wont, I promise.

FOLA: Goodbye, mum. I love you.

SADE: *(controls her tears as she waves at each of the children.)* I love you too. I love all of you! *(Everyone begins to cry as Fola goes to lead the rest of the children who are waiting at the entrance of the house.)* I'll come for you very soon! *(She begins to shed much tears as she leaves the place.)*

SCENE FIVE

(Bosede and Junior are both reading in the sitting room when there is a knock on the door.)

BOSEDE: Who's it?

SADE: *(from outside.)* It's me, Mama Seun.

BOSEDE: *(looks at Junior.)* You can go and open the door for her.

JUNIOR: *(goes to open door and prostrates before Sade.)* Welcome, ma.

SADE: *(smiles at him.)* Hello, Junior. *(He helps her with one of her bags. Bosede goes to meet her at the door.)* Hello, Mama Junior.

BOSEDE: *(smiles at her.)* Hello, Mama Seun. Are you traveling?

SADE: Yes - sort of... but I need to see you first.

BOSEDE: *(frowns.)* Where are you packing to?

SADE: I'm packing out of the town for good...

BOSEDE: *(looks at Junior.)* You can excuse us. Go to your room and complete your home work. *(While Junior leaves the room with his books, she gestures Sade to have her seat. Both of them sit on the couch.)* What's happening?

SADE: As you are aware of my new life in Christ, I have to make a restitution by putting the wrong things right. Of course, I know I cannot possibly amend all the wrong choices I have made which cost my sister her life. Since God have used Miss Benson to make me realize that Nuru is not my husband, I have to live him.

BOSEDE: Does it make much difference if you leave him?

SADE: Yes, of course. At least, I have God to please. That's all that count, isn't it? If I don't have any man to marry me, so be it. What else do I need? I have children and I have Jesus who is more important to me than life. As I read it in the Bible, Jesus said we should not fear those who can kill the body and nothing more. We should rather fear God who can kill the body and cast the soul into lake of fire. I'll rather go through the hell in this world than to go through the one in the lake of fire.

BOSEDE: That's very courageous of you. You seem to have counted the cost.

SADE: *(nods.)* Yes, I have and I'm ready to pay.

BOSEDE: How about your children? And that of your sister. They all count on you to survive under the circumstances they find themselves.

SADE: That's one of the reasons I've come to see you. *(She is full of emotion that brings tears into her eyes.)* I need your help.

BOSEDE: You know I'll do anything to help if it is within my power. What do you want me to do?

SADE: I want you to persuade your husband to talk Nuru into bringing the children here.

BOSEDE: It took the power of God to break the union between the man and my husband. I really don't want my husband to have anything to do with him again. I do hope you understand.

SADE: *(frowns.)* No, I don't. Perhaps if you explain I may understand you.

BOSEDE: *(shrugs.)* You remember the occultist brothers you told me about the other time? *(Sade looks thoughtful as she reflects the day, nodding.)* My husband eventually joined the cult despite all I did so to stop him. Just recently, he told me how the cult tries to initiate Junior.

SADE: What?! *(She jumps on her feet impulsively and sits down again.)*

BOSEDE: It's a long story. The way God intervened in my family made my husband surrendered his life to Christ. He told me it's your husband that took him in. He told me all kinds of atrocious acts that are more than enough to cause a nightmares. Ever since then, he's been growing steadily in Christ. Associating with your husband can...

SADE: It's okay. I understand. You have to protect your home.

BOSEDE: That's right. But because I can't just leave all the problems to you alone, I'll go and persuade him by myself.

SADE: You're not in the position to do that. He knows we're friends and he'll know I ask you to come.

BOSEDE: He'll still know you send us even if I get my husband involved. I think we should pray about this and ask God to direct us on how to bring them here. I'm sure God will not leave the problem for us to solve. He'll do something about it, especially when he knows we are trying to do his will.

SADE: I must confess to you that God have already begun the miracle. I was forced to make the confession to Fola, the first child of my sister. He proved it to me that he's a real Christian when he said he loves me in spite of what I did to her mother. He said they have been taught at the fellowship of the need to always forgive and forget about any wrong that are done against them.

BOSEDE: *(looks impressed.)* That's a wonderful beginning of restitutions. I can now see what Miss Benson means when she said parents risk too much by not putting the spiritual lives of their children into consideration when planning for them. It's not enough to put them into schools with high academic standard. Their total well beings must be balanced with the word of God. Take a look at my son, Junior who tackled the cult with the power of God. I thank God for the life of Miss Benson who brought Jesus into this house. If not for that, my son would have been initiated into secret cult at that age right under my roof at young age.

SADE: That reminds me. Do you think any of my children is a member of a secret cult?

BOSEDE: How am I supposed to know that? What I can say in that regard is that if the children are here with us, we can influence them to renounce it. We'll all be going to Church and learn the word of God together.

SADE: Then you have to do all you can to get them to stay with you - please. *(She goes on her kneel.)*

BOSEDE: You don't need to do that. With God on our side, with God on our side, we'll bring them here.

SADE: *(sits down.)* Thank you so much. *(She is moves to tears.)* To have a trusted friend like you gives me strength and encouragement, which I desperately need to carry out the decision to obey God in this matter.

BOSEDE: We thank God for everything. Where do you plan to go now?

SADE: Honestly I don't know yet. But I know if I have to do this, I have to do it alone. The only thing I know is that God will order my step. Since I don't know where the Lord will lead me, I don't have answer to the question. I will contact and inform you of my location from time to time. You and Miss Benson are the only ones I can trust with the information about my movements.

SADE: *(signs and nods with understanding.)* Okay.

SCENE FIVE

(Days later, Nuru sits at the veranda of the house with a bottle of hot drink in his hand. Fola comes out of the house, going to him.)

FOLA: Dad, there is no more raw food in the house.

NURU: *(in a drunken and harsh manner.)* So what?!

FOLA: I need some money to go and buy the items.

NURU: *(takes out some money in his pocket and hands it over to him.)* Here. That's all I've got and that's all you'll get.

FOLA: *(counts the money silently and looks at him.)* This is not enough to buy half of what we need.

NURU: *(gestures him to leave.)* I told you that's all I've got. So get the hell out of my sight!

FOLA: *(hesitates for a while.)* But why, dad?

NURU: Why what?

FOLA: Why don't you give Jesus a chance in your life? You need him desperately.

NURU: Who is Jesus to a Muslim? He's a minor prophet! I'm a Muslim - a real Muslim. My name is Nurudeen.

FOLA: Dad, we both know you're not even a real Muslim. The life of a Muslim is not like this. It's more descent. *(Nuru stands up to slap his face but he moves backward a little. He misses and goes to sit down again.)* We really have a problem in this family.

NURU: You better shut up your dirty mouth. What do you know anyway?

FOLA: Dad, there is no need to pretend as if I don't know anything about what you did to my mother and my aunty who became my step mother. Don't tell me that's the life of a Muslim.

NURU: *(frowns.)* Who told you that story?

FOLA: That is not question we are supposed to ask. The question is: is it true? *(There is silence between them as Sade and Kola enter the compound. He looks at them. Fola goes to greet and lead them to him.)* **You!** *(Nuru points at them in a drunken manner.)* The enemies of the brothers have come to see me - huh? To laugh at me that my wife left me? *(Kola and Bosede quietly go to join him.)*

KOLA: We've come to help you, Nuru.

NURU: I don't need your help. I can handle the situation very well.

BOSEDE: Baba Fola, it's never too late for God to save you if you give your heart to Jesus now.

NURU: *(stands up chummily and points at her.)* If you dare tell me about Jesus here, I'll deal with you ruthlessly.

KOLA: It's okay, Nuru. *(There is silence.)* Can we help you with the children?

NURU: How?

KOLA: I mean we want to take them away.

NURU: Where do you want to take them to?

KOLA: They'll stay with us since their mother is not around to look after them. *(He looks at Fola.)* Would you and the rest like to follow us?

FOLA: Yes, sir, it dad approves it.

KOLA: *(looks at Nuru.)* Do you approve it? *(Nuru waves impatiently.)* Does that mean yes?

NURU: Take them if you want. They are bunch of pests in my life anyway.

KOLA: *(looks at Fola.)* You and the rest of the children can go and pack your things. We'll take you with us when going. *(He looks at Bosede.)* I'll like to talk to him alone. You can go and help the children pack their things. *(Bosede frowns.)* You can trust me with this, my dear. *(She shrugs, smiles and then goes inside the house.)* Nuru, you may not be in the mood to hear this truth but I still have to say it so that it'll be in the record of God that you were told the truth. *(Nuru waves indifferently.)* Since the incidence that made the Brotherhood to kick me out of the group occurred, my life is never the same. As we both witnessed God demonstrating His great power through my ten year old son, we both have reasons to turn our lives over to Jesus, the Son of God who died on the cross for our sins. He rouse up on the third day to proof to the world that He is the promised Messiah. If you accept Him as your Lord and Saviour now, the three things that take place in your life will also happen in your life too. First of all, the blood of Jesus will wipe away all your sins, no matter how much they are. Secondly, you will be delivered from the power of sin with the peace of God reigning in your life. Lastly, you will have hope of eternity in heaven when you die in this world. *(Nuru shrugs indifferently.)* My friend, let me tell you something about death as we read it in the Bible which most people are ignorant of. There two types of deaths. Funny enough, what human calls death is not really death. It is called sleep. The first type of death is spiritual. If you don't have Jesus who gives life in your life, you're a spiritually dead person. If you die physically as a spiritually dead person, you will find yourself in the lake that burns with fire and brimstone, which according to Revelation Chapter 21 Verse 8 is called second death...

NURU: *(bursts out laughing.)* You too have been programmed like the fanatics! *(Kola signs and shakes his head sorrowfully.)*

SCENE SIX

(Few weeks later, Fola is reading the Bible at Kola's house while everybody including Kola, Bosede, Junior and the rest of Nuru's children listen.)

FOLA: *"... And as if is appointed into men once to die, but after this judgment."*

BOSEDE: *(looks at the book and the Bible in her hand.)* The passage in Hebrew Chapter Nine Verse Twenty-seven tells us of the judgment day that will come one day. *(She looks at the book in her hand.)* I'll read what we have here in this teaching manual. *"Have you noticed that there is always a dash between the date of birth and the year a person dies on his tomb inscription or in the obituary notice? The dash is actually a question about whether he or she is really dead or asleep at the bosom of the Lord?" The answer to the question of life and death is determined by how the person lives his or her life. Is the life full of righteousness or unrighteousness? Holiness or unholiness? Obedience or disobedience to the word of God? Light or darkness? Acceptance or rejection of Jesus Christ." (She looks at Fola.)* You can read he book of Revelation Chapter Twenty-0ne Verse Eight.

FOLA: *(opens the Bible and reads.)* *"But the fearful, and unbelieving, and the abominable, and murderer, and whoremonger, and sorcerers, and idolater...* *(Kola's phone begins to ring. He looks at it and goes outside to receive the call while Fola continues to read.)* *...and all liars, shall have their part in the lake which burns with fire and brimstone: which is the second death. (Kola comes inside, looking very gloomy while Fola is still reading the Bible. Bosede looks at him.)*

BOSEDE: *(looks inquiringly at him.)* What's wrong, honey?

KOLA: It's a... *(He goes to whisper to her.)* It's really bad news. Nuru is dead. he had an accident.

BOSEDE: *(screams involuntarily.)* Jesus!

EPISODE THIRTEEN
TOTAL DELIVERANCE
SCENE ONE A

(Miss Benson is writing a note from a book in the office when the door is knocked. She looks up.)

MISS BENSON: Please, come inside. *(Fola in his school uniform comes inside the office, looking gloomy.)* Hello, Fola.

FOLA: Good afternoon, ma.

MISS BENSON: *(gestures him to a seat.)* Please, have your seat. *(Fola sits down quietly. There is a brief silence.)* Joe delivered my message to you?

FOLA: *(nods silently.)* Yes, ma. He told me at the fellowship yesterday that you want to see me.

MISS BENSON: Yes. *(She leans backward.)* Everybody at the school fellowship observed that you've lost your joy since you lost your father. *(She pauses.)* I didn't observed this each time I come to your School Fellowship and when I visit you at Mama Junior's house. Can you tell me what exactly the problem is?

FOLA: *(looks reluctant.)* I just feel we are alone with no family - no father and no mother. None of our family members are in the town.

MISS BENSON: You know Junior's family is also your family.

FOLA: Yes. The family members are really doing their best but I just feel we are too young to face this kind of problems. To add more to it, mummy didn't come to pick us as she promised when we went for my father's funeral in our hometown.

MISS BENSON: You can't blame her for that. She told me what she is going through. According to her, when she got to Abeokuta, she had to live almost like a vagabond after she spent all she had with her. She faithfully attends one Church where she was made to understand that it was not easy to do the will of God. People who have lived wrong life for a long time would find if difficult to live right but your mum is determined to do the will of God. It was huge sacrifice for her to leave you but it's going to pay off at the end of the day.

FOLA: How?

MISS BENSON: *(smiles at him.)* According to what she told me, she had a three day fasting and prayer....

SCENE TWO

(Bosede is in the church alone kneeling in front of the alter, praying, weeping and singing.)

SADE: *It is well*

With my soul
It is well, it well
With my soul.

Lord, I have gone this far with you... Deliver me, Oh Lord. I plead for your mercy in Jesus name! I need you to give me a job that will earn me enough money to look after my children and that of my sister's. I know I don't deserve anything from you but think of the blood of Jesus that was shed on the cross of Calvary for my sake and tamper justice with mercy, Lord. *(She sings again.)*

The blood of Jesus
The blood of Jesus set me free
From sin and sorrow
The blood of Jesus set me free....
His name is higher
Than any other name
His name is Jesus
His name is lord...

SCENE ONE B

MISS BENSON: It was a very fervent and effective prayer. She told God to remember her as he remembered Joseph in the prison and as he remembered Hannah who was barren. Don't forget she was only asking for a job that would earn her enough money to take care of you. God visited her right in the Church that day which was the last day of the personal prayers and fasting...

SCENE THREE A

(Sade is still praying in the Church when Olamide drives a jeep into the premises, gets down from the car and goes into the Church. Bosede is still praying inside when Olamide enters and goes to sit down, looking at her. As she sings and prays.)

SADE: *I love the man*
Of Galilee for he has done
So very much for me
He has forgiven me all sins
And send the holy Ghost to me
I love that man of Galilee

Lord, all I need from you now is a job. *(She begins to cry.)* If you give me a job, I'll get enough money to look after my children and that of my sister's and I will praise your holy name.

I have seen Jesus
I have seen Jesus deep in my heart
He's more than my man.

104

(As she stands up, she opens her eyes and sees Olamide. She looks startled.) Oh. My God! *(He smiles at her and moves closer to her.)*

OLAMIDE: I'm sorry if I interrupt you.

SADE: *(shrugs and smiles.)* It's okay, sir. I suppose you've come to see the Pastor.

OLAMIDE: Oh, no. I've come to see you.

SADE: *(looks puzzled.)* Me? *(He nods, smiling at her.)* There must be some mistakes somewhere. You probably take me for someone else.

OLAMIDE: Not at all. I've been praying for something for a long. God told me in the dream that the thing I've been praying for is in this Church. So I came here. *(He looks around.)* I suppose this is em… All Saints Gospel Church?

BOSEDE: Yes, sir.

OLAMIDE: I've been looking for this Church two days ago until I got it now.

BOSEDE: What is that thing you're looking for?

SCENE ONE C

FOLA: *(frowns at Miss Benson.)* Who is the man?

MISS BENSON: The man is an industrialist.

FOLA: I see.

MISS BENSON: What do you see or guess?

FOLA: I guess he wants to employ her.

MISS BENSON: That's a good guess but let me continue with her testimony before I tell you her plans for you and the rest of the children.

KOLA: *(nods vigorously.)* Okay.

MISS BENSON: *(looks thoughtful.)* The man started telling her about himself after both of them have settled down to talk…

SCENE THREE B

OLAMIDE: *(sits a little closer to Sade.)* My name is Olamide. I'm addressed as Deacon Olumide because that's what I am in my Church. I'm into the production of foot wears and textile materials.

SADE: Oh, thank God! God has sent you to employ me in your company?

OLAMIDE: Hold it, sister. I wasn't praying for an employee because I don't really need any for now. I have enough if not more than enough.

SADE: *(looks disappointed.)* Oh… *(She looks hopefully at him as he smiles.)* How about employing me as your house help? I can do any domestic work for you.

OLAMIDE: *(smiles again at her.)* I don't need house help either.

SADE: Then why did God send you to me?

OLAMIDE: If you give me time to explain, you'll understand,

SADE: Okay. I guess I am too eager to get a job.

OLAMIDE: I understand that you're a child of God, aren't you? I heard you praying desperately for a job. When I entered, you concluded that I came to give you a job. As a child of God, I expect you to know that God doesn't give remnants to his children. If you ask God to give you a shelter, he will give you a home. If you ask for water, he'll give you a river. Jesus said if human beings know how to give good gifts to their children, how much more God who gives abundantly.

SADE: What does God plans to give me now? I've waited for so long for miracle and my children are suffering.

OLAMIDE: God understands what you're going through but you need to understand also that there are processes to get miracles. If God plans to give you anything, he ensures that what he gives you would not get into your head. You see, God makes the people of Israel to go through wildness for so long for just one crucial reason. The experience in the wilderness is to make them understand that man should not live by bread alone but by every word that comes from God. Whatever you have gone through in life is not meant do crush you but to rather build you.

SADE: Okay, I understand.... But I'm running out of patience. I hope God have not sent you to tell me to continue going in this wilderness.

OLAMIDE: No. Before I tell you what I believe God has for you, I want you to confirm if you're married or not.

SADE: I'm ashamed of my past. Telling you the truth can make you change your mind about what God wants you to do for me.

OLAMIDE: *(smiles at her.)* Have you heard a song like this before? *(He begins to sing.)*

　　　　　I'm not moved by what I see.

SADE: *(sings with him.)* Hallelujah!

OLAMIDE: 　　*I'm not moved by what I hear*

SADE: 　　　　*Hallelujah!*

OLAMIDE: 　　*Come on, let us*

SADE & OLAMIDE: *Amen, amen, amen, amen!*

SADE: *(hesitates for a while.)* I'm not really married.

OLAMIDE: I see. But you have children.

SADE: That's the ugly part. I had children. The father of my children is my sister's husband.

OLAMIDE: *(smiles.)* That's what makes you ashamed.

SADE: *(in a whisper.)* Yes...

OLAMIDE: As far as God is concerned, you're not the one that commits the sins. Since you've been forgiven, God overlooks the days of your ignorance.

SADE: You're the fifth person to say that. Thank you for reminding me of that.

OLAMIDE: Is that all you want to tell me about yourself?

SADE: Well... Em... My sister killed herself because I got pregnant by her husband. I stayed in the house to have more children and look after my

106

sister's children. After I gave my life to Christ, I left the town to begin new life. So I need a job before I settle down and bring all my children with me.

OLAMIDE: I can see why you're so desperate to get job. You think so many things depend on it. Right?

SADE: Yes, sir.

OLAMIDE: *(signs.)* I lost my wife two years ago.

SADE: Oh, I'm so sorry....

OLAMIDE: It's okay. She's with the Lord. That's something to rejoice about. So many things are going wrong in my home and at work. So I prayed to God to give me a wife. He told me in the dream that my wife is in this Church. He said I'll find her praying here.

SADE: *(looks stunned.)* Y'you mean God says I'm going to be your wife?

OLAMIDE: *(shrugs.)* Yes. You have the Spirit of God. So you can confirm it from the Lord if you don't believe me.

SADE: Y-you don't understand, sir. I mean I may not be worthy to be your wife.

OLAMIDE: What do you mean by that? Who is worthy of who? Is there anyone who is worthy of Jesus among any of us? Yet He came to die for us. Remember this: we are all from the dust and into the dust we shall go. Death is the proof that we are all equal before God. We shall all die one day - no matter who you are - males, females, rich, poor people. Only Jesus makes us worthy to inherit the kingdom of God.

SCENE ONE D

FOLA: *(looks happy.)* Wao! Did mummy accept his proposal to marry her?

MISS BENSON: I know you'll ask me that. *(She pauses.)* She called me on the phone on the day the man proposed to her and asks me to pray along with her. I did and God confirmed it to her Pastor shortly before the death of your father. The good news now is that they are going to get married quietly - very soon.

FOLA: What does that mean?

MISS BENSON: It means they won't make noise out of the wedding. They'll pay the dowry to the family of your mother. They would go to registry for the marriage.

FOLA: The marriage may be too quiet for a man like that.

MISS BENSON: You may be right but, according to the Pastor, that is the way God wants them to do it. Besides that, marriage is not the noise you make out of it but the peaceful union, harmony, love and unity between the husband and the wife.

FOLA: *(looks happier.)* I'm so happy today.

MISS BENSON: *(smiles at him.)* I know. You can tell the rest of the children the good news.

FOLA: Why didn't mummy tell me this before now?

MISS BENSON: They gave me the honor to break the news to you.

FOLA: Thank you so much, ma. At last, we'll have something to rejoice about.

MISS BENSON: Thank God for everything. Let's pray before you go. (She begins to pray.)

SCENE FOUR

(Kola and Bosede are watching the television with the children when a car parks in front of the house. The doors are opened. Sade and Olamide come out of the car, going towards the house. Inside the sitting room, Fola looks through the window.)

FOLA: *(looks excited.)* They are here! *(The rest except Kola and Bosede crowd round him.)*

THE CHILDREN: *(in diverse ways.)* Mummy! Welcome!

KOLA: *(stands with Bosede when the couple enters.)* You are welcome.

BOSEDE: *(looks at Olamide kneels.)* You are welcome, sir.

OLAMIDE: *(bows.)* Thank you, ma. *(He shakes hands with Kola who offers his hand.)* I'm Olamide.

KOLA: Deacon Olamide. *(He smiles at him.)* We already know so much about you.

BOSEDE: *(looks at Sade.)* What takes you so long?

SADE: We have to see Miss Benson and the Pastor before coming here.

BOSEDE: I see. I know it's getting too late to travel down to Abeokuta but you still have to take the meal we prepared for you.

SADE: We've been eating since… Oh, let me officially introduce you to my husband. *(She gestures at Olamide.)* This is my husband. *(Olamide nods at the couple. She gestures at the couple.)* These are Mr. and Mrs. Olaosebe. *(She points at Junior.)* That's their son, the young pastor in the house. *(Junior prostrates to him.)* His name is Kolade Junior. *(Olamide goes to shake his hand. She looks round at the rest.)* I guess you already met the children before. Since we are now married, they are officially your children now.

OLAMIDE: Yes. *(He looks round at them.)* I am very glad for today. I'm filled with joy in my heart. Well, as you all know, we've come to pick the children just as you have approved. But first, let's take this moment to appreciate God for all he has done by thanking and praising Him for a moment. *(He begins to sing. The rest join him.)*
    We are grateful, oh Lord…

SCENE FIVE

(Each of the children goes to hug and say goodbye to Kola, Bosede and Junior before going into the car.)

BOSEDE: I'm going to miss you children.

THE CHILDREN: *(in different ways.)* We'll miss you too.

JUNIOR: *(looks unhappy.)* Would you always come and spend your holiday

108

with us?

SADE: I'll come and take you to spend holiday with us. You need to give your mum and dad time to make another child anyway. *(All the adults laugh. Olamide goes to shake Kola.)*

OLAMIDE: Once again. Thank you, my brother.

KOLA: Thank you also for all the gifts, sir.

OLAMIDE: It's nothing. God will bless you more than this. *(He looks at Bosede.)* The Mother of many children. Thanks a million times for being there for your friend, my wife.

BOSEDE: Thank you too, sir. *(Olamide and Sade get into the car.)*

SADE: *(smiles and waves at them.)* Thank you again. *(As the car drives out of the compound, the two families waves at each other.)*

EPILOGUE
A CALL TO A DUTY

Everyone had at one time or the other made a mistake. Therefore, no one is in the position to blame anyone for anything because we are all ignorant of different things. However, we have a duty to educate each other on what is of mutual benefits. The fact is: we all contributed to what is happening around us either through sheer ignorance, negligence or even arrogance. I often tell people when holding seminars that if they don't train their children in the way of the Lord, someone or something else will model them in the way of the world. Parents have placed too much of their future in the hands of others by concentrating only on the academics and welfare of their children, neglecting their moral values that can make them responsible. This makes many of them educated members of secret cults, armed robbers, prostitutes and agents of fraud.

The family and moral values of most of the children had been destroyed. Out of sheer sexual excitement, a lot of children are born and bred in poverty. While looking for a way to survive, these young ones ventured into stealing. They soon they graduate from stealing into robbery or fraudulent practices like the notorious 419 scam. If we start tracing the societal problems from parents as we see it in the episodes of drama, we will appreciate this fact better.

As parents, we have a duty to our children and make them good citizens. As school teachers, we must impact moral values in our students. As a researcher and writer, I have a duty to educate and share my findings on the cause of social vices. As patriotic citizens, we all have collective responsibilities to make positive impacts in the life of others either through contributing positive things into their lives, encouraging or educating them on things that will add moral values into their lives.

On this note, I wish to introduce to individual, the family, school, Churches, campus and other Fellowships Calvary Rock Resource books, that are showcased in the next few pages.

I wish to appeal to you also to help us fight the vices in our society by either hosting, funding or fostering the establishment of Bible Clubs or Fellowships in your school or your children's school.

Thank you for taking time to study the results of research into social vices in these episodes of drama.

- Pastor Dipo Toby Alakija

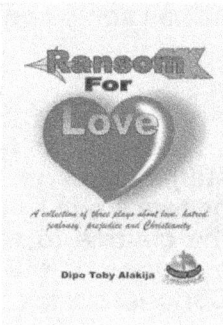

111

Because she considered the proposal to marry him as a marriage engagement with the devil incarnate, she decided that she would rather die than to share her life with him. Then out of the blues, this passionate gentleman sneaked into her life despite all she did to discourage him. She could not resist his love for her when he offered to set her free from the devil incarnate. Then the battle began – sooner than they anticipated.

NO MORE TEARS TO SHED
ISBN: 978-49874-3-0 ISBN: 978-978-74-3-1
Kidnappers took Tokunbo away from his grand parents in a city in Nigeria when he was a little boy. A nice woman found him in another town and gave him a false identity. She spoilt him with love, making him to grow into a rebellious teenager that was not appreciated anywhere. When Janet made him a Christian, however, life began to make sense to him until the day he was beaten to the point of death for the offence he knew nothing about. He left the town for the city which, unknown to him, held his true identity and the link to his parents in the United States. To find them was only a question of time.

THE UNROMANTIC LOVE BIRDS
ISBN: 978-4987-5-7 ISBN: 978-978-4974-5-5
And other short stories about love and marriages
They were very much in love right from their school days but when they got married and had children, romance became the game Charles' wife refused to play. No matter how much he tried to make her understand the unbearable condition her unromantic attitude has subjected him into, she would not change. Consequently, after enduring for so long, he was forced to look for the women that would make up for her weakness. He unofficially married a beautiful lady of insane jealousy. Though she was ready to give him what was missing in his marriage, it soon dawn on him that he has solved one big problem only to create a bigger one.

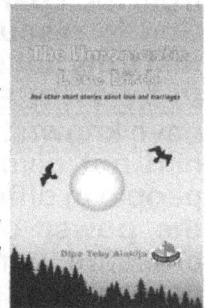

THE BATTLE OF THE CONQUERORS
ISBN: 978-49874-7-3 ISBN: ISBN: 978-978-49874-0-7-9
Wickedness takes over the land of Bondage from First Couple and subjects everybody into slavery without giving anybody the chance to be free. Love brings The Redeemer from Eternity and offers the slaves the chance to escape. Wickedness soon declares war and engages everyone in the battle. The Redeemer makes the redeemed people Conquerors by giving them the armour of war and Comforter but

Wickedness cannot be undone. He has several thousands of years of experience in the war. So he is quick to recognize the weakness of the redeemed people who are ignorant of their strengths and advantages. Although the Conquerors fight like immutable giants, rescuing victims of war, many people suffer heavy casualties.

Since King Wickedness knows that a redeemed person is strong enough to chase one thousand of his warriors at a time, and two would put ten thousand into flight, he enlists as one of his warriors the people's deadliest enemy called Disunity.

Wickedness is able to strike the people by making them to fight with one another, turning what is supposed to be their best moments in the battle into tales of woes.

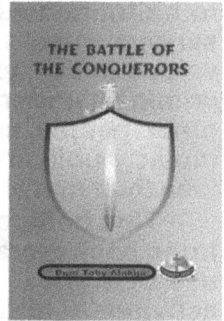

BLOODSHED IN CAMPUS
ISBN: 978-07350-3-8 ISBN: 978-978-07350-3-6

A poor widow tearfully warned her son, Richard, against joining the bad wagon when he got an admission into one of the Nigerian Universities. He resisted the membership of groups of students, including the Christian Fellowship until he had an encounter with a member of The Black Skulls - a deadly and ruthless secret cult on the campus.

Before Richard knew what he was up against, the head of The Black Skulls had arranged items for his initiation into the cult. While resisting being initiated, he ran to the Christian Fellowship for help. The leader of the Christian Fellowship dragged The President of Students' Union Government (S.U.G) into the conflict. With the involvement of the S.U.G President, another formidable cult called The Red Eyes felt obliged to team up against The Black Skulls. Then the campus turned into a battlefield and BLOODSHED became the order of the black day.

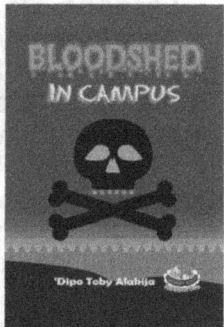

NETWORK BIBLE CLUB
YOUTH AND ADULT BOOK ONE
ISBN: 978 - 978- 49874-9-X ISBN: 978-978-49874-9-3
A collection of 26 life transforming stories, 26 poems, 26 hymn tuned songs and weekly Bible lessons

The issue of moral instructions in schools and at homes is threatened with extinction. Consequently, so many youths are involved in prostitution, drug addictions, cultism, fraudulent practices, armed robberies and other crimes. Those who are supposed

to be trained as leaders in various walks of life are the ones posing serious threats to many lives. Many parents who fail to add moral values to the upbringing of their children often times breed potential criminals under their roofs without knowing it. Apart from these, many other people negatively influence young ones through the media, music, publications, films, conduct and foul language; making them to lose their moral and family values.

This book one just like the rest of other volumes is an attempt to bring back moral instructions into schools and campuses through the use of stories, hymn tuned songs, poems, Bible lessons and class activities. It is designed to assist teachers and ministers in Secondary Schools, Bible Clubs, Churches and Campus Fellowships to teach people, especially youths the Word of God and serves as a school text book in subjects relating to literature, music and other creative works.

FOUNDATION BIBLE CLUB A-Z STORY BOOK
ISBN: 978-49874-2-2 ISBN: 978-978-49874-2-4
Volume 1 With 26 Stories, 26 Bible Lessons, 26 Rhymes And 26 Songs For Book For Young Minds

An adage says, "a man who builds a house without building his child builds what the child will later sell." Proverbs 22:6 says, "train up a child in the way he should go: and when he is old, he will not depart from it." This book is an attempt to assist parents and teachers to meet up to the challenges that befall them in carrying out this important function in the light of the moral decadence that is prevailing all over the world.

The first edition of the book was used by several thousands of teachers, ministers and parents in schools, Churches and homes to build the moral values of young ones. Apart from the stories, songs and Bible passages for the young ones to study, there is a seminar material that is based on the lecture which the author delivered to school proprietors, children ministers and Christian professionals in this volume.

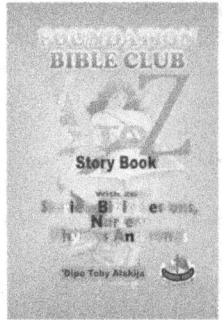

SUCCESSFUL CHRISTIANITY AND BASIC MINISTRIES
ISBN: 978-49874-6-0
A Collection Of Resource Materials That Precedes Christian Ministries And Basic Leadership Course Book

The first question is how Christianity is practiced even in a hostile environment. Next to that is the question about the potentials of Christians in spite of their apparent limitations. The other issues are connected to the successes, deliverance, callings,

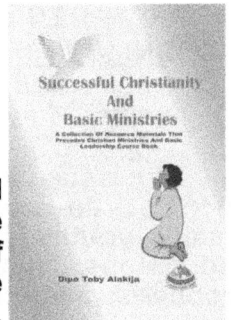

basic ministries of all Christians and evangelism. Various schools of thoughts have attempted these questions but many answers only portray Christianity as a form of religion instead of a way of life as specified by God. Some answers give room for compromise, hypocrisies, dogmas and denominational doctrines. The misconceptions about these areas of Christianity have brought about worldliness instead of righteousness and false achievements instead of fulfillment.

This book which contains six different subjects had been used to hold seminars at various levels, train ministers and Christian workers in Bible Schools and to equip the Church. It explains in simple terms the seemingly complex issues on practice of Christianity, Potentials, Deliverance, God's Kind Of Success, Evangelism and Basic Ministries of a Christian with Biblical principles, life transforming stories and illustrations.

CHRISTIAN MINISTRIES AND BASIC LEADERSHIP
ISBN: 978-36348-7-9 ISBN: 978-978-36348-7-9
A Collection Of Resource Materials That Follows Up Successful Christianity And Basic Ministries Course Book
As it is common to say that the hood does not make a monk, the dignified positions and bogus titles of many Christian leaders in modern days do not really make them Gospel Ministers.

This course book - a compilation of five resource materials on Missions And Outreach Ministries, Christian Communication Arts, Christian Leadership, Christian Education Methodology and Ministries Of Improvisations - aims at making every matured Christian an effective minister and leader at their respective homes, communities and nations. It teaches various ways Christians can communicate the word of God, meeting up to their responsibilities as ministers and leaders that reconcile people to God, edifying the Body Of Christ and reaching out to souls at the same time.

All of the resource materials are in use in Bible Schools like College Of Christian Education And Missions, in Churches and other ministries to raise Christian workers, Evangelists, Missionaries and other Ministers that serve at various levels and leadership capacities.

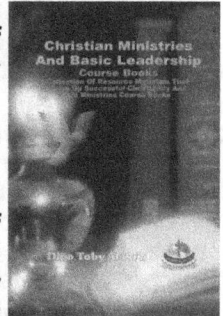

INSANITY OF HUMANITY
ISBN: 978-36348-6-0 ISBN: 978-978-36348-6-2
The Results Of Research Works Into Various Methods Of Brainwashing
Man is made to exercise his freewill. The mind of his own and the power to choose between right and wrong, good and evil, light and darkness is about to be washed away through brainwashing. The

agents of control dubbed as Secret Government by John Todd (the top Illuninati defector) have put necessary machinery in place to ensure that all human beings are in conformity in their thinking and ways of life, trying to wipe away diversity, which makes each person unique.

This book attempts to shed light on how the techniques of mind control are applied through the use of propaganda, education, entertainments, drugs, religions, media and other means of communications. It is the result of research works, some of which are based on findings of various researchers and writers like Bugger Lugz, Edward Hunter, Hadley Cantril, Herbert Krugman, David L. Robb, Vaughan Bell, Juliana Gomez, Ryan Duffy Vice, Henry Makow, David Nicholls, Fritz Springmeire, Steven Hassan, Renate Thienel, Debra Pursell, Mary Pride and a host of others who are acknowledged in this book.

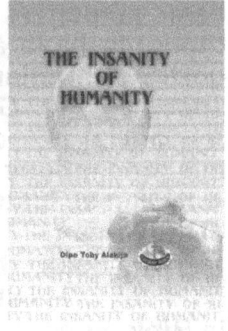

CALVARY ROCK RESOURCE BOOKLETS
ISSN: 1595 93X
The Quarterly Missionary Booklets That Are Designed To Teach Children, Youths And Adults In Schools, Fellowships, Churches, At Homes, Office And Other Places.

Although all the various volumes of this booklet can be used independently of other books but it is recommended that it should be used as part of supplementary materials to make up for Foundation and Network Bible Club Story Books for both children and adults in School, Church, Campus, Office and other Fellowships.

Each of the volume is rich with quarterly Bible lessons, stories, drama, songs, seminar, tract materials and a host of other things that can be used to edify, educate, entertains and evangelize every category of people, ranging from children to elderly persons.

Every volume is designed to equip school teachers, ministers in Churches or campus or office fellowships and other people who wish to work with the Lord.

All These And Other Books Are Distributed Worldwide And Published By The Publishing House Of Calvary Rock Resources

*Ikenne-Remo, Nigeria
*Manchester, United Kingdom
*New York, United States

www.calvaryrock.org